TRANSCENDING

Beyond the illusion of self,
to the reality of what you are

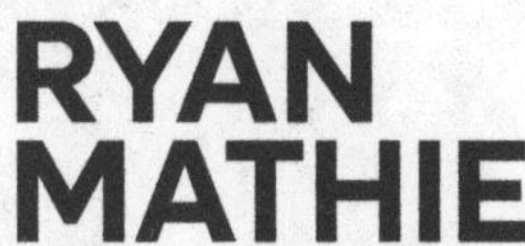

Rethink

First published in Great Britain in 2026
by Rethink Press (www.rethinkpress.com)

'The deepest possibility for a human being is to wake up from the illusion of a separate self.'

— Ryan Mathie

Contents

Introduction

The journey of a seeker often begins without warning. Something shifts, something breaks, and what once made sense no longer does.

For some, it arrives as a sudden awakening – so clear and powerful that everything changes in an instant. For others, it comes gradually through life's challenges and hardship: the slow disintegration of a former life; the grief of losing what once defined them; the collapse of imagined identities constructed for safety. Years of repeating familiar and destructive patterns, facing fears, failures, hopelessness, depression, or profound loss can eventually lead to surrender. The need to control can no longer hold up the weight of pretending and the old self begins to give way. In that space, something deeper begins to emerge. Consciousness rises from within.

The problem of the mind

The mind doesn't see clearly. It filters life through threat, fear, memory, and conditioning. It attaches, resists, judges, and tries to control. In that endless distortion, it finds problems that don't actually exist. It builds a false identity that we call 'I'. Even our effort to go beyond it – through therapy, spiritual practice, ceremony, or self-improvement – can unknowingly reinforce it.

Many sincere seekers stay stuck or simply keep on searching not because they lack commitment, but because they haven't fully seen through the workings of the subtle, refined ego. The false identity they adopt may be of someone 'doing the work', 'awakening', even of 'the teacher', or 'the one who knows'. Until it is clearly seen, it continues – disguised, refined, convincing, alluring, 'successful', popular, renowned, spiritualised, but still false. This is the mind trying to solve its own problem from within itself – like attempting to illuminate the sun with a flashlight.

For those who hear the call to end the search and who commit themselves fully to the path, the journey becomes one of highs and lows, and ongoing transformation. The illusions of the mind dissolve, layer by layer. Each release brings greater clarity, peace, and alignment with what is real. Progress may not always feel obvious in the moment, but over time the shifts become undeniable. Life becomes the teacher, revealing exactly what needs to be seen with perfect timing.

The most devoted seekers don't walk this path for attainment. At some point, truth becomes the only thing worth living for. Old patterns of thought become obvious and less tolerable. Anything misaligned with our essence begins to register as distortion – like a frequency that no longer fits. There's a relentless search for answers, guidance, and support. The movement is instinctive, as if being led by something greater than ourselves. There is a silent recognition, a light in the distance leading the way – a knowledge without language.

The approach to dismantling the illusion of self and realisations shared in this book is modern, practical, and born from direct experience – not from religious doctrine, philosophical abstraction, theory, conceptual understandings, blind faith, or borrowed ideas. It did not arise from following any lineage, pre-defined path, or established teaching, but through the raw meeting with life, the unravelling of distortion, and the living recognition of truth revealing itself.

This book as your guide

Humanity's deepest evolution is the dissolving of illusion and the return to our true nature – not as separate individuals, but as expressions of one living field. No system, method, teaching, technology, or spiritual performance can deliver it, though they may point. It's recognised as what's already here: the stillness beneath thought, the presence beneath identity, and the love that needs nothing.

This evolution is not outward. It is inward.

This book is a guide through that inner return. It offers clear, direct principles for meeting what arises, dissolving the distortions that obscure truth, and seeing beyond the identifications of the illusory self-image and the limitations of the mind. It points to the clarity, freedom, and peace of awareness itself – the reality that has never left, waiting to be recognised beneath all that was once believed to be real.

This work is advanced only in this sense: it is for those who are genuinely committed to truth over comfort, identity, or the illusion of safety. For those willing to meet the deepest layers of themselves, face whatever arises, and walk the path with devotion and humility. For those who have explored, questioned, healed, and grown – yet sense that something essential is still missing.

It can also meet someone at the beginning, but only when they are already pulled by something deeper – a genuine draw towards truth itself. Without that sincerity, the work will not land.

The practices and clarity shared here will meet each seeker exactly where they are. Nothing is offered as belief; everything is meant to be tested directly. Take what resonates and discard the rest. When the moment is right, the right thing always lands. There is no movement to join, no belief system to adopt, and no 'way' to follow. This book makes no claims of ownership – only an offering. It points, simply and clearly, to what is already here, beneath the noise of the mind. Truth does not belong to anyone. What's shared here is not mine, and it is not yours. It is what it is.

Through the practices and pointers shared throughout this book, it becomes possible to dissolve illusions, clear emotional and energetic blockages, and open the way for a higher intelligence – whether you call that God, Source, or by no name at all. What's revealed isn't a better self – it's the seeing that the self that could be improved was the illusion.

And when that lands, suffering can end.

This book wasn't written from a mountaintop after everything was complete; it was written inside the journey, as part of it. Many of the truths in these pages were clarified and confirmed in real time, through heartbreak, solitude, nature, family, and the refining that followed. I include personal stories throughout as real moments that illuminate key stages of this unravelling. In that sense, the book has been my teacher as much as it is a guide for you – a living record of what life has revealed and continues to reveal. Even as these words are written, subtler layers of identity continue to unwind. This is not the voice of arrival, but of ongoing exposure.

It unfolds in three parts:

- **Part One: The Call To Come Home** explores the discovery of the Transcending practice, the nature of consciousness, and the core obstacles that obscure direct knowing.
- **Part Two: Transcending** presents simple but powerful practices for dissolving identity, releasing resistance, and aligning with truth at source.
- **Part Three: The Evolution Of Consciousness** shows what becomes possible when this practice is embodied – both individually and collectively.

Each part builds upon the last, offering not just understanding but a direct path to lived realisation.

Transcending is a solitary inward journey, yet it is universally available. It offers a direct way to return to peace, presence, and truth. This book is a clear, precise, and contemporary guide for that return – pointing not to something new, but to what has always been right here all along.

Many of these insights have been pointed to across cultures and traditions for centuries; what follows is how they were seen and realised here.

Let us begin.

PART ONE
The Call To Come Home

Every spiritual journey begins with an irresistible call back to truth. For many, this call is not new. Steps have been taken, insights have come, and moments of deep clarity may already have broken through and yet, that which is being sought may not have fully revealed itself.

Part One of this book traces the journey from the first encounter with consciousness to the discovery of Transcending, and lays bare the source of human suffering: the mind's mistaken identity as a separate self. Such a self is fictitious.

When illusion falls away, there is nothing to be attained. This is the call to come home – not for the first time, but more completely – to the truth of what we are, beyond name, label, or role: pure being.

1
The Journey So Far

In nature, animals align with an unseen intelligence that guides their survival, showing them where to go and how to find what they need. A flock of birds or a school of fish, moving as one, or ants working in union for the good of the colony – all seem miraculous. Beyond the mind's overlay, this same collective intelligence is orchestrating humanity on a grand scale.

At first glance, the human journey appears chaotic, messy, and filled with struggle or even devastation. It often seems as though something is fundamentally wrong and life should be different, but this interpretation comes through the filter of the ego-mind, born from misidentification and a false sense of separation.

In reality, the human experience, with all its trials, complexities, and horrors, unfolds exactly as it must within the larger context of evolution. Every individual journey is reflected on a grand scale and is intricately woven into the whole, each one contributing to a greater unfolding. What we see 'out there' serves only to show us what's 'in here'. Nothing is separate. Life – personal, collective, and beyond – is a single, perfect expression of divine intelligence in motion.

Much like a seed buried in the soil, undergoing countless mutations before it grows and blooms into its fullest expression, humankind also undergoes the experiences needed to grow and evolve. It could be said that what we're seeing now is simply that evolution becoming more visible.

The mind often judges humanity harshly. Yet, we are much like a young child still learning to walk. In the vast timeline of the planet, humans are relatively new; we are still stumbling, falling, and making mistakes along the way. Like any determined child, the human species is persistent, destined to find its balance and grow. In time, it will learn to walk and then run, embodying more of its full potential to mature, thrive, and expand. This movement mirrors the life and journey of a seeker.

The ordinary view of life is from a point so close to the canvas that the full painting stays unseen. Stepping back reveals undeniable progress. From centuries of war, conquest, genocide, and slavery, the trajectory has gradually shifted from the dark ages towards more integrity, freedom, equality, and human rights. Though slight, slow, and often brutal, history suggests an ongoing evolution towards higher levels of consciousness and points to what humanity is at the core, beyond the mind: integrous, authentic, responsible, accepting, loving, compassionate, humble, kind, gentle, and forgiving, experienced as an ever-increasing sense of togetherness.

The global, historical shift mirrors the individual experience. Reflecting on the personal path of any seeker taken so far reveals a clear pattern of growth. Every step, every mistake learned from, every challenge overcome, every act of kindness and forgiveness, contributes to the whole. Progress that is made individually, affects the collective. When intention and commitment align with this natural evolution, the unfolding continues with less effort and more flow, guided by that very same intelligence that orchestrates all of life.

This one intelligence, consciousness, has always been present, directing humanity towards its truest and highest expressions. However, egoic illusions rooted in fear, resistance, and separation block the truth, perpetuating cycles of suffering and division. Like a dusty mirror, these illusions reflect reality, but obscure the truth – until it is cleared by the light of awareness.

Consciousness is never absent, only illusion seems to block it. Eventually, though, even the deepest shadows dissolve in its presence, and what has always been true is revealed.

A first opening

For me, the journey began in a fractured home, shaped by insecurity, survival, and a deep feeling of 'not enough'. Years were spent seeking love, success, and meaning outside myself, only to discover that none of it could truly satisfy.

At thirty, with no spiritual background or preparation, a spontaneous and irreversible shift occurred. Walking through the streets of East London, consciousness exploded into awareness. The false self dissolved temporarily. Life would never be the same.

Around that time, I had just entered a new relationship, and every weekend my partner and I argued. She would pull away for no clear reason, and I would be hurt, get angry, and push for resolution. We replayed the same loop for four weeks straight. Then one day, while walking through Bethnal Green, she turned to me and said, as she had many times before, 'Ryan, it's nothing to do with me.'

For the first time, something in me paused. A new question appeared: *What if this has something to do with me?* It's funny now, but at that point the thought had never once occurred to me before.

I had spent my whole life believing I was right about everything, blaming others, blaming life, blaming circumstances, but all that really mattered to me was the truth. In that moment, everything shifted. My entire life flashed before me – broken relationships, family conflict, failed projects, every time something hadn't worked – it was me there all along. I was the single consistent factor. I felt dizzy, like I might collapse. I went home, fell on the bed and cried for hours. First with grief – thirty years of believing my own illusions. Then with liberation – because for the first time, I was beginning to see through them. Life was never the same.

The very next day I wrote a long list of things I had done that I was not proud of and started to clean it all up. I contacted ex-partners and apologised. I called my family and asked why we never said 'I love you', and why we never spoke honestly about our past. We had real conversations for the first time. They were deeply moved, shocked, and terrified all at once – this wasn't our usual kind of catch up. They suggested I see a psychologist but to me, everything made sense. I hadn't been living in reality. I was waking up from a long sleep.

Humbled, though, I followed their advice and visited a psychologist. I shared with her everything that had transpired in those past couple of weeks – what

I'd seen, what had opened up, what I had already resolved within me and with others. She was shocked at first, then settled into disbelief. She told me she'd been working with patients for two decades and had never seen or heard of anything like this before. She was frank with me – she thought it was an act and suggested I return the following week, an invitation I respectfully declined.

Instead, I spent the next two years going deep on my own, adding to my list until it was complete. I cried most nights but woke up with even greater clarity each morning. It was intense and liberating. There was no one in my life at that time that would understand what I was going through, so my sharing of this journey was cautious and selective.

Finding a guide, becoming a guide

Eventually, someone did hear my story. She suggested a course that gave language, further clarity, and a completely new edge to what I'd been experiencing on my own. Soon after, I left a high-paying consultancy job, joined that very training organisation, and quickly became one of their senior leaders. I had entered a unique world of responsibility, integrity, and seeing through stories. I was held accountable every day. It wasn't just about cleaning up the past anymore; it was about living differently *now*. I cried regularly from the pressure and the terror of being called out. All the old stories – 'not good enough', 'can't do this', 'not possible'

– were being pulled to the surface and stripped away. It was intense, gruelling, and unlike anything that had come before. I kicked and screamed most days but in spite of the pressure and confrontation, I absolutely loved it. Nothing mattered more to me than the truth.

After five incredible years in that world, I knew it was time to move on. So, without a plan but full of trust, I left.

Expansion

A few years later, after building a successful independent coaching practice and working with a wide range of personal and professional clients, I co-founded and led a training company dedicated to supporting other coaches and personal development professionals. Leaders came to me to break out of limiting beliefs, dissolve emotional blocks, and create the kind of deep, lasting results they had experienced first-hand in our work together, so they could offer the same transformation to their own clients.

I developed and trained them in a process I created, called Unshakeable Belief, reflecting the level of insight I had reached at the time into how beliefs form and dissolve and, essentially, how to make things happen and be unstoppable.

Some part of me sensed that there was something beneath it all that remained incomplete, but compared to what I had been practising before, the results were extraordinary. I went on to teach this process to experts and leaders across the world, many of whom brought it into their own client work. The principles became part of their foundation and to this day, many still use that very training to support deep and lasting transformation in others.

During a five-year period, we directly served over 7,500 transformation coaches, executive coaches, therapists, healers, spiritual teachers, and personal development experts, and through them, thousands more were reached via an exponential ripple.

Eventually, though, I surrendered even this role. I realised that this kind of success could not give me the peace and happiness I was looking for, so I let it all go. The company, the labels, the status, the possessions, the striving, the security, and any relationships that were no longer aligned – I let go. What was left was a clearing – free of the noise and void of distraction – where truth could finally be met as it was. This book is the fruit of that journey. Sixteen years of persistent undoing with a single intention: everything false must be seen through and let go. Truth is all there is.

Discovering Transcending

The foundation that this book is built upon didn't arrive all at once. There were countless movements that contributed to its discovery, but a few key moments marked the early turning points. The first real glimpse of what I would later refer to as 'Transcending' came during a trip to the US. I had a severe toothache, and nothing was relieving the pain, so at around 3 am I gave up trying to escape it and intuitively decided to sit with it, in meditation pose – no resistance, no avoidance. I dropped into the centre of the pain. Within minutes, it began to dissolve and I fell asleep. The pain left, but the clarity stayed.

Around the same time that I began building the training company for personal development leaders, I ended a long-term relationship and noticed something strange – I didn't cry. I knew I was sad, but no grief came. Something didn't seem right. I came to realise that while I had been focusing so much on mindset, shifting beliefs, and creating results, I had unknowingly cut myself off from the deeper emotional layers. I could grow a company easier than I could feel. I could create wealth and lead thousands and yet I couldn't sit peacefully in silence. The contradictions became clear, and slowly my awareness started to shift further inward.

Years later came the moment that took it even deeper. Since moving from Scotland to London at the age of twenty-one, I'd developed a silent fear of losing my mum and had been avoiding examining it for years. She was my safe place in a chaotic childhood. When COVID-19 hit she was alone, and I worried for her. The fear reached a point where my awareness could finally meet it. After all these years, I realised I had to face what I had been repressing. Intuitively, I lay on the bed, closed my eyes, and let the fear come. I didn't resist or fight it; I let it flood me. Grief, panic, sadness, love – it all came. I cried for hours and when it was done, the fear and grief were gone. It had lived in me, utterly suppressed, for two decades, and in one night, it dissolved. I felt light and connected to something far beyond the mind but I had no words for it. It was a mystical experience that felt new and known all at once. Rumi pointed to this kind of experience when he said, 'The wound is the place where the light enters you.'[1]

Rude awakening

The next realisation on the way to discovering Transcending came during a relationship that was full of fire, passion, and drama – a rude awakening of sorts. It was an intense connection that became the catalyst for so much that would unfold. By then, I could recognise that my partner had an avoidant attachment style – she was distant, uncommunicative, and needed lots of space. With my anxious attachment style, I was triggered constantly.

After one argument, I promised not to push her boundaries. Hours later, she shut down again. I reached for the door to go after her, then stopped.

I had made a promise, and I could do nothing but honour it. Instead, I had to literally force myself to walk away and I locked myself in another room. I thought my head was going to explode with anxiety and somehow knew that this was it – I had to face it. I was terrified.

Intuitively once again, I sat in the meditation position and let myself feel what was there. It shot through my system like a rocket. As I allowed it to rise, emotion erupted like I had never felt before. As the emotions intensified, old memories surfaced: being left with my dad as a kid, feeling unsafe, looking out the window and up the street waiting for my mum to come back. I let myself see it all and remember. I connected with that memory of my younger self and allowed the emotion to move through me. I cried extremely hard and then… silence, lightness, total stillness.

The formation of my anxious attachment pattern was seen, understood, felt, and – in some major way – released, in a matter of minutes. A specific pattern that had haunted me for years dissolved in one seemingly miraculous experience and never came back. In that moment, I set a profoundly clear intention: to complete my past and remove every obstacle to peace. I pictured what that would mean, and what it would take to remain in such a state, so that nothing could trigger me. It felt like a bold and deeply right intention – one that set a new course and would change everything.

Synchronistically, during this same period I encountered the teachings of Dr David Hawkins. He talked about enlightenment and consciousness in a way that struck a deep chord and resonated with what was already coming through, yet something in me knew it was not the time to explore other people's ideas; I had to go deeper on my own. Presence was leading, and I could feel it. Instead, I bought Hawkins' full collection of books and set them aside, trusting I'd know when the time was right.

The clearing

When that relationship ended, devastation and heartache followed. While many expressions of my anxious attachment had by that point dissolved, the deeper root had simply found a new form within this relationship. But this time, there was clarity – and I finally knew how to meet it. The light of awareness within was coming on brighter and it was clear that there were more deeply hidden layers of emotion, buried tension, unresolved pain, programmes, and patterns than I had previously realised. They were all waiting beneath the surface, ready to be seen – and I was ready to see them, no matter what or how long it would take.

Before anything else, I had to face this heartbreak. I cleared my calendar for a week, turned off my phone and sat with the unbearable truth: it was over. For a solid five days and nights I did nothing but sit and observe, feel, allow, and release. Over and over. Stories, illusions, fear, sadness, clinging, heartbreak, attachments – all of it passed through and out, and in its place came wave after wave of emotion, release, clarity, peace, wisdom, insight, and indescribable revelations.

I would sit sometimes for hours at a time. I could feel something – a presence – was awakening inside of me. There was no pull towards seeking external help – only a deep need to sit in silence and the knowledge that this part was to be walked alone. It felt right, and completely natural. At the very bottom of this unravelling, like finding a needle in a haystack, I found something unexpected – a well-hidden programme: a belief that my happiness was almost complete, but not quite. I was 99% full on my own, but the final 1% would only come through being in a relationship.

That idea – created in childhood, influenced by movies, cultural stories, and collective conditioning – had shaped so much. But none of it was true. Happiness wasn't missing anything – it was already here. When I saw through that particular illusion, the grasping for another person instantly disappeared. The pain dissolved and with it, other hidden beliefs began to unravel. It was like pulling a key piece from a stacked game – everything else collapsed around it. That moment broke the spell, but the pattern itself would need more time to fully complete.

I felt so free and so light – like I was levitating. My mind was completely silenced. I felt clearer and cleaner than I had in over a decade's worth of intense personal work. No blame, no shame – just truth. The challenges revealed in this relationship had shown me exactly what I needed to see to evolve. Everything was perfect and had to happen exactly the way that it did – I was simply grateful.

Touching source

For the first time, I felt the undeniable and inexplicable direct connection to what I can only describe as source. I had been an atheist my whole life, but this was different. I could feel the intelligence behind it all – consciousness, presence, awareness, divinity. It wasn't separate from me; it was both within and without. There was no separation, only an unbroken interconnectedness. Life wasn't happening *to me* – it was moving *through me*, through all of us. I was left speechless, sitting in complete silence. No words were needed. This was a state beyond anything I had experienced before, a sense of inner peace that could not be described.

Wisdom and clarity continued to pour through me – I felt completely plugged in. At that point, it became clear that this was never about escaping, shifting, or conquering the mind, but about seeing it exactly as it is, without being pulled into its stories or the futile effort to construct better ones.

I felt the emotions fully, letting them be there. I gave them space, lots of space, and in that space the truth revealed itself on its own, in its own time. I didn't rush it or resist it, even when it was uncomfortable. As the obstacles began to dissolve, wisdom emerged, and what I really am was becoming even clearer.

After each wave passed, I felt more of my essence and deeper nature. More light, more presence, more love, more peace, more calm, more stillness. The practice was obvious and simple: observe, feel, allow, release. Feeling and allowing needed plenty of time and patience, releasing seemed to happen mostly on its own, but I knew I had to be willing.

This was the moment it all connected. The first opening had come all those years ago in the US, in the dissolving of physical pain, and then in Bethnal Green with the release of life-long grief, the dismantling of anxious patterns – and now this. Heartbreak, and multiple life-long patterns surfaced and began to dissolve in a major way. The obstacles were never problems – they were doorways. The practice wasn't a rigid method; it was sitting with life, as it was, and letting it show me the way home.

Coaching no longer resonated and came to a natural end. I began sharing the practice in the same way that I had guided myself. I ran small retreats, special online events, personal one-on-one and small-group immersive experiences where people could sit in silence, observe, feel, allow, and release. Presence naturally unwound what the mind could never touch.

People went deeper than they ever had before, clearing life-long hurts and unwinding deeply ingrained patterns by simply closing their eyes and meeting themselves fully. Other experts wanted to learn how to guide their own clients, and I ran a one-off pilot training course. It was successful, and the experience was beautiful, but something felt off. The way forward hadn't fully revealed itself yet, but I could sense it wasn't that.

Answering the call

I sensed this was the beginning of something even deeper. Instinctively, I knew I had to pull back from every distraction and allow space for whatever wanted to come through.

Eventually I sold or gave away all my possessions – property, car, belongings. The luxurious life I had built – at this point on the island of Madeira, Portugal – was released, piece by piece. It was time to lighten the load, to let go of everything, every tie, every role, every identity that no longer belonged. My outer life began to reflect the clearing that was unfolding within.

Though I stepped away from the business I co-founded and led for five years and paused most public work, a few remnants still played out – a final offering, a project that carried the residue of the old world. However, the ambition and identity that had once driven it all began to dissolve, and it became increasingly clear that none of it could continue. Life was guiding me towards solitude and, eventually, I disappeared from public life entirely.

There was no strategy, no 'what's next' – only stillness, flow, and life living through me. A complete retreat unfolded. I spent months at a time in ashrams, meditation centres, conscious communities in Europe, and the jungle of Central America, with occasional visits back to my family home. I lived free from distraction and the mind's direction. Along the way, I met people whose presence and reflections helped me see what I was ready to see. I rested entirely in being, mostly on my own and for periods in complete silence.

What needed to come through could only emerge in emptiness – and slowly, it did. The path was revealing itself. I didn't yet have the words for it, but I knew I was being drawn to the very heart of what I had been seeking all along.

Yet the stillness didn't erase what had been buried. In the quiet, the mind's patterns became even clearer. Unresolved and extremely subtle programmes surfaced. Old identities tried to reassert themselves. Without the noise of daily life to hide it, I could see how suffering operates and stays intact – not as a random force, but as a predictable outcome of how the self-structure works.

If I was ever to realise true liberation, I knew I had to face that inner machinery head on. No more chasing highs, no more hiding in ideas of bliss. What was required was a willingness to meet the subtle, persistent ways the mind keeps control, to face all my fears and attachments, and to stay with it all until it burned itself out. I devoted every waking moment to this, until there was nothing left to hold onto. I did not yet realise that what I was looking for would reveal itself most clearly through the accumulation of moments after seeking stopped and the usual filters fell away.

Summary

The journey I have described so far shows that obstacles and patterns are not barriers but doorways. Each layer that dissolves brings forward more of what is real. What feels like struggle or heartbreak is in fact clearing the way. At the heart of it all lies a profoundly simple practice: observing, feeling, allowing, and releasing. This practice reveals that peace, clarity, and the love that all seekers are looking for, are not found out there but have always been present within. Life is not working against us; it is always guiding us home.

2

Suffering And The Ego: The Internal Struggle

Stillness brings clarity, but it also removes the hiding places. Without the noise and distraction of daily life, the mind's movements become easier to see. Old identities surface and familiar emotional patterns try to pull attention back to the story. The suffering they create is not random – it follows a clear design.

At the centre of this design is the ego: the mind's image of itself, referred to as 'I'. It is built for survival from memories, beliefs, and conditioning, all woven into a sense of 'me' that must be defended, improved, or protected. Left unseen, this identity filters every experience, shapes every reaction, and reinforces the illusion of separation.

To be truly free, it is not enough to chase moments of bliss, peak spiritual experiences and emotional highs, or to temporarily distract the mind. The deeper work is to observe the false self in real time, see how the machinery of suffering operates, and allow it to dissolve in awareness. This chapter explores that machinery, explains how it keeps us stuck, and shows why facing it directly is essential to lasting freedom.

The construction of the ego

Longstanding contemplative traditions have always described the ego not as a physical entity, but as a process: a pattern of identification with thought. The inner controller isn't something you can point to or locate in the brain. It's a habit of attaching to thoughts, beliefs, memories, and imagined identities about who we think we are. This view is consistent across various traditions, including Advaita, Zen, early Buddhist psychology, and modern phenomenology, and is pointed to in the teachings of Sri Nisargadatta Maharaj and David Hawkins. [2,3]

In its earliest form, the ego was a survival mechanism, helping early humans secure food, avoid danger, and protect the body. But as physical threats became less constant, the ego didn't disappear – it adapted.

No longer focused solely on ensuring a body's physical safety, it turned its attention inward, protecting not a person's life itself, but their sense of self: a mental image built from past experience, memory, social feedback, and imagined futures. This is where the split began. What once served to ensure survival now served to protect a fragile and entirely fictional identity.

From the moment we arrive in the world, our self-image begins forming. At first, it's shaped by the people around us. We learn our name, what gets us approval, and what gets us in trouble. We notice which emotions are welcomed and which cause discomfort in others. Every smile, frown, or moment of silence leaves a trace.

We don't just take in rules and behaviours; we absorb the emotional charge that comes with them. If anger is punished, it might be pushed deep down and hidden away. If achievement brings love, then striving becomes second nature. These patterns sink into the body, shaping the way we hold ourselves, react, and move through the world.

Over time, the self-image is reinforced through family expectations, cultural norms, and life experiences. It can appear confident or insecure, bold or cautious but at its core, it's nothing more than a collection of remembered experiences, decisions, and fixed and inherited ideas.

The imagined separate self builds roles to protect itself and to keep this image intact. Roles like:

- The high achiever who believes their worth depends on constant progress

- The caretaker who suppresses their truth to feel needed
- The victim who clings to pain to justify their circumstances
- The rebel who defines themselves by opposition and resistance
- The perfectionist who fears being exposed or not in control
- The fixer, who believes wholeheartedly in their responsibility to save others

As the journey progresses, the identity often becomes more refined, taking the shape of the teacher, guide, seeker, or even the wise one. It carries an image of being spiritual – grounded and insightful in conversation, still and serene in meditation, fluent in scripture and spiritual language, fluid on the yoga mat, possibly dressed in robes or mala beads, adorned with tattoos, feathers, crystals, or other symbols of depth. The vocabulary shifts toward 'energy', 'alignment', and 'truth'. The bookshelf fills with the 'right' authors, and the lifestyle becomes an act of purity. On the surface it can look impressive, even awakened, but often beneath it endures the subtle hold of a fictional self – an identity built around the idea of being someone who 'knows', and in some cases, someone who has already 'arrived'.

The patterns and roles aren't 'bad' in themselves – they begin as ways to navigate the complexities of life. The problem comes when we believe they are *who we are*. Then they shape how life is interpreted, how others are related to, and how freedom is postponed.

The truth is: the controller (ego) is a mental construct. Seeing it clearly is not about destroying it, but about no longer needing to be a 'someone' at all. Beyond all roles and patterns there is a natural presence and freedom that has never lacked anything, never needed to become anything, and simply is as it is – beyond what the mind can grasp.

How the ego generates suffering

The Buddha, in the *Dhammapada*, stated: 'From desire springs grief, from desire springs fear; free of desire, there is no grief – how then fear?'[4]

This points directly to the core mechanism of suffering. When there is desire – whether for approval, control, security, status, or love – it creates a dependency on certain conditions. If they are met, there is temporary relief. If they are not, the result is fear or grief. The personal self lives through this mechanism, constantly chasing what it wants and resisting what it doesn't.

Suffering, therefore, isn't random. It follows a predictable pattern – one the ego repeats over and over. It is trying to protect the self-image it has built. It wants to be seen a certain way, to succeed, to avoid rejection or failure. These are not personal flaws – they are inherited survival programmes. As long as the persona is running the show, desire persists, and fear and grief inevitably follow.

The mask is constantly measuring, comparing, and defending. It scans for threats to what it desires, including physical safety, and anything that could challenge its sense of self. A look, a tone of voice, a lack of recognition, a change in plans – all of these can be read as a personal attack and be threatening to the identity.

This is why so many reactions feel automatic. An offhand comment can trigger a wave of anger or shame before there's even time to think. The mind immediately produces a story: why they were wrong, why we were right, why we need to explain, fix, defend, or attack. Each story tightens the knot, keeping the emotion alive.

The inner narrator thrives on this cycle because it confirms the belief that the self-image is real and must be protected. But the more it resists, the more suffering it creates. Every attempt to control how life unfolds, or how others see us, becomes a point of friction against reality. Most people, without realising, swim upstream and wonder why they feel like they're drowning in life.

Lao Tzu captured it well in the *Tao Te Ching*: 'The ego is a monkey catapulting through the jungle: fear and grasping, branch to branch, never resting.'[5]

The truth is: life isn't attacking us. It's simply moving. But to the ego, anything that doesn't match its idea of how things should be feels like a threat and so is resisted – that resistance is where suffering begins.

Suffering can take many forms – frustration, resentment, fear, anxiety, loneliness. But the core is always the same: identification with the mind's version of events, and with the false self it creates, rather than seeing reality as it is – attachment and resistance.

The cost of living from the ego

So as we see, living from the imagined self comes at a high price – not just in moments of obvious conflict, but in the background of daily life.

When the self-image is in charge, every interaction becomes a subtle negotiation for safety, approval, or control. Conversations are filtered through the question: 'How does this make me look? What does this mean for me?' Even moments of joy are fragile because they depend on things going a certain way. Over time, this creates an underlying tension – a constant readiness to defend, prove, or secure the identity. It can feel like being on high alert without knowing why. The body holds the stress while the mind rarely rests.

Relationships suffer because they're never truly free. Every connection is shaped by expectation and comparison. We unconsciously seek validation and avoid rejection, which keeps love conditional and guarded.

The same pattern touches purpose and money. Work becomes about proving our worth, meeting expectations, or securing our safety, rather than an expression of what feels true. Money shifts from being a practical tool to a measure of value, success, or security – always tied to the ego's sense of self.

Life lacks ease. Instead of moving with what is, we're always leaning into the next problem to solve, the next thing to gain, the next way to avoid loss, the next self-improvement to make. Even when things are good, there's the familiar hum of 'what if it changes?', 'what if something goes wrong?', 'what's next?' It's madness and it is exhausting.

The real cost isn't just stress or unhappiness – it's the disconnection from reality itself. We stop experiencing life directly. Everything is filtered through the mind's narrow lens and with that filter, peace is always out of reach and real happiness becomes a 'someday, one day, when…' event.

Mastering the illusion versus living the truth

In today's world, many have mastered what is regarded by most as success: attention, identity, visibility, and wealth. Some build entire lives around perfecting their self-image, curating public identity, and bending perception. In a culture that rewards visibility, fame isn't a byproduct – it's often *the* product.

Much of what's built serves people. It inspires, uplifts, even creates genuine impact but behind the contribution is often a more subtle game – one where identity is tightly held, carefully managed, and constantly maintained.

Even in the spiritual and intellectual worlds, the ego dominates and evolves into highly refined forms. It wears wisdom as a brand, dresses stillness as a persona, and packages presence into product. Teachings are polished, scaled, marketed, and distributed. The words may remain true, but the living transmission that once pierced illusion often reduces under the weight of the structure that forms around it.

The larger the audience grows, the more money there is to make, the harder it becomes to see. Roles solidify and personas embed deeper – the image must be sustained. The illusion of grandeur and the pressure to be a special someone becomes the fuel that keeps the identity alive.

What begins as genuine clarity can easily turn into performance and the more convincing the performance, the more the world rewards it – with recognition, authority, influence, financial gain, and cultural status. But beneath the surface, the loop is still the same: perform, maintain, protect, adapt, repeat.

What looks like transcendence is often the high-functioning version of the same game – identity dressed up in more sophisticated clothing. The identity structure does not disappear; it simply evolves into something harder to recognise. This identity may look enlightened, peaceful, or wise but as long as it depends on maintaining an image, protecting a role, or sustaining a structure, it stays rooted in the illusion of an individual, separate self.

The real shift is not about building a better identity. It's about seeing through the structure altogether. Not with rejection or bitterness, but through simple clarity: there was never anyone here to perform in the first place. The self, however convincing it appears, is a fiction.

The perfect hiding place

Modern life doesn't make it easy to see this truth. The pace is relentless – work, bills, kids, family, the constant ping of notifications. Days become a blur of commitments, tasks, and screen time. Even moments that could be spacious are filled with distraction. There's little room to pause, to notice, to feel, or to simply rest in the moment. It's a jungle out there and it is very noisy.

Emotions don't vanish in this busyness – they get buried. We learn to push them down so we can keep moving and keep functioning. The strain builds gradually; the mind stays busy solving the next problem or chasing the next milestone, while the body carries the weight of what hasn't been felt.

This is the perfect environment for the false self to stay in charge. The busier life is, the easier it is to mistake the mind's constant commentary for reality, and the harder it is to remember what's underneath it all.

It doesn't only happen in the chaos of everyday life. The ego hides just as easily in spiritual spaces. Here, the distractions are found in teachings, practices, ideals, and medicine. The search for truth itself can quickly become another distraction, addiction, and a way to feel special, more advanced, or 'further along' than others. Spiritual language and concepts can mask the very patterns they're meant to dissolve, creating an identity of being someone who is 'awake' or 'on the path'. In these spaces, the self can hide in plain sight, disguised as devotion, wisdom, or service. At this point, we can notice just how sophisticated and intelligent the ego actually is – subtle enough to weave itself into even the most spiritual of pursuits, clever enough to survive no matter what. It is quite striking.

But regardless of its effort to stay hidden, for a seeker of truth, one way or another, reality catches up with the inner manager. We can avoid examining the illusion for a time, distracting ourselves with work, relationships, success, constant activity, and endless books, teachings, gurus and retreats. But eventually, life presents situations that bring the inner conflict to the surface and our sense of self to our knees. These moments can be uncomfortable, painful, even humiliating, usually ending up in some kind of burnout. Life says: 'Stop. Look. Listen. See the illusion and let it go.'

We can't hide from life – it will always bring the reflections needed to reveal what's been hidden. Nothing stays buried forever. Peace doesn't live inside performance or the roles we play. It begins the moment the mask is seen for what it is, when the endless effort to *become* is no longer needed, and all that's left is the return to *just being.*

The possibility beyond ego

The good news is that, while the ego is not who or what we truly are, it is not the enemy. It formed to protect us, to make sense of experience, and to create strategies for survival when there was no other way. It served a purpose. But what once kept us safe eventually becomes the very thing that limits us. The structures that helped us adapt are the same structures that now obscure what we really are – and like any construction, they can be deconstructed.

When even a small gap opens between awareness and thoughts, something shifts. We begin to notice that the voice in our head isn't actually 'us' – it's a running commentary, shaped by the past, predicting the future, defending the self-image. In that moment of noticing, the grip of the ego begins to loosen.

Within this space, life is no longer filtered through the question of, 'What does this mean for me?' Each moment can be met directly as it is, without pretence or defence. With sincere dedication, and over time, the confinement of the old self-image falls away and what is left is a freedom and happiness that is real, lasting, and was never outside of ourselves.

Beyond the ego, there is a reality that isn't dependent on circumstances. Emotions still arise, challenges still appear, but they move through us without defining us. Life begins to be lived from clarity and flow, rather than from the push and pull of identity.

This is the opening that leads to the rest of the journey – it's not an escape from the reality of life, but a truer way of being in it.

Summary

The ego is not a 'real' thing but a pattern of identification that shapes how life is seen and lived. Left unquestioned, it generates suffering by filtering every moment through the lens of 'me', creating tension, resistance, and separation. Yet the same patterns that create struggle also hold the key to freedom, because when they are seen clearly, they begin to dissolve. Beyond the roles and stories lies a stability that has never been and cannot be broken. The journey ahead is about uncovering that steadiness and learning to live from it, so that life is no longer defined by illusion but revealed in truth.

3

Beyond The Illusion Of Separation

At the heart of the human condition is the (false) belief that we are separate – separate from each other, from the world, from life, and from Source, from the Creator – that which many call God. This belief is so deeply woven into the fabric of our minds that it rarely gets questioned. It is the background assumption from which almost every pattern, thought, feeling, and action arises.

We grow up in a world that confirms this separation at every turn. We are taught that we are individuals, moving through life in our own separate bodies, with our own separate minds, each of us needing to secure 'our' place in the world. We compare, compete, protect, defend, and strive – as if we are isolated fragments, trying to survive and succeed on our own.

This illusion of separation fuels the survival self by feeding the endless cycle of resistance, judgement, blame, and fear. It makes us believe we must fight to be safe, prove ourselves to be worthy, and seek externally what we already are. It is the source of the suffering that permeates every layer of life – personal, collective, and spiritual.

And yet, we are not separate.

The root of the illusion

The illusion of separation begins early. From the moment we open our eyes, we are met with a world of forms – faces, voices, colours, and shapes. Slowly, the mind learns to divide up and label this world: 'me' and 'not me', 'mine' and 'yours', 'good' and 'bad'.

As children, these distinctions help us navigate life. We learn that our body is ours, which toys are ours, which food is ours. But over time, these labels harden into identities. We also absorb the patterns of separation inherited from our parents – their fears, their beliefs, their strategies for surviving, and ways of relating. The mind becomes convinced that 'I' is only this body, this mind, this story, separate from everything and everyone else.

This is the seed from which the identity grows. Once we believe we are separate, life becomes about protecting 'me' and managing the world 'out there'. Relationships become a trade of needs and fears, and 'love' becomes a survival strategy. Success becomes a way to secure perceived worth. As mentioned, spirituality too can become another way of seeking validation and approval, trying to fill the illusory gap between ourselves and the source of all existence.

The problem is not that we have a body or a mind, but that we mistake them for what we truly are at our core. This case of mistaken identity as a separate self is the engine driving all of human suffering.

The world as a mirror

Once the illusion of separation takes over, the outer world begins to reflect this back at us everywhere we look. Life becomes a series of encounters that seem to confirm that we are distinct, incomplete, and in need of something to make us whole.

Relationships and loneliness mirror our insecurities. Success and failure mirror our self-worth. Conflict mirrors our hidden fears and unhealed pain. Even moments of joy are overshadowed by the fear that they won't last, will be taken away, or the silent guilt that we somehow don't deserve them.

This can feel like punishment, but it's a perfect feedback system. Life reflects what is held within, offering constant opportunities to see the false self at work. But what feels like an attack, rejection, or loss is often a doorway – a chance to meet the part of us that believes it is separate and in danger.

Without reflection, the illusion could remain hidden indefinitely. Yet life does not make it easy for us to stay blind forever. The same patterns circle back again and again until they are finally seen and released – or else they continue, repeating right up to the death of the body. But one way or another, sooner or later, the illusory self will die.

The cost of separation

Living from the illusion of separation means carrying a constant, subtle tension. It's the background undercurrent of needing to secure, defend, and prove an identity that was never real in the first place. This tension shows up in countless ways – anxiety over the future, regret over the past, comparison with others, and a never-ending fear of not being worthy or enough. It affects every layer of life.

The cost isn't just emotional or mental; it's physical. The nervous system stays on high alert, with the body carrying the weight of unresolved emotions and constant self-protection. Over time, this erodes vitality and joy, giving way to exhaustion and disconnection.

In this way, the illusion of separation is the root of all suffering. The more tightly the false self is held onto, the more life is experienced as something to manage, fix, endure, or control, rather than something to be lived fully.

The split and the search

The moment the mind begins to identify with the body, a split appears. Life is no longer experienced as one seamless whole, but as 'me' and then 'everything else'. This shift is subtle and universal, and goes unnoticed. The natural sense of being dissolves into a constant inner commentary, dividing reality into subject and object, self and other, here and there, before and after.

Once the split has occurred, the search begins. We start to look for belonging, love, safety, and meaning as if they are somewhere 'out there', separate from us. The more we search, the more we reinforce and sustain the sense that what we need is missing from us and that what we are is not enough.

The tragedy is that what we are searching for has never been missing, yet the mind, being addicted to movement and 'progress', fails to recognise stillness and presence as the answer. Instead, it creates a new moving target, projecting happiness onto the next achievement, the next possession, the next teaching, the next relationship. Like a mirage in the desert, it shimmers with promise in pursuit but then disappears the moment it is approached. The cycle of longing, grasping, and temporary relief continues; it is relentless and exhausting. This whole endeavour is endlessly complex and yet, ironically, reality itself could not be simpler. What the mind is chasing in a million directions is already here; it was here long before the searching began and will be long after it ends.

The self-image makes us believe we are either too small or too important, but both extremes come from the same illusion of separation. True understanding reveals a deeper paradox: the dissolving of the personal self and the recognition of the field as one.

As Nisargadatta Maharaj put it: 'Wisdom says I am nothing. Love says I am everything. Between the two my life flows.'[6] In other words, when the separate self drops, nothing is missing and nothing is excluded.

Division everywhere

The illusion of separation and the endless searching it triggers isn't just a personal experience – it's the filter through which the collective sees the world. It shapes culture, politics, religion, education, and even the way we relate to the planet. Every system built on the fundamental belief in a separate self carries the same signature: division, control, greed, cruelty, obsession with safety at any cost, and the endless pursuit of 'more'.

Nations are divided by borders, beliefs, and resources, convinced that survival depends on defending what's 'ours' from 'them'. Religions fracture into denominations, each claiming exclusive truth while missing the deeper unity that birthed them all. Even well-intentioned movements for peace, justice, or change can become entangled in the very patterns they seek to dissolve, fuelled by opposition and fear rather than clarity.

The same dynamic plays out in everyday life. We compare, compete, and curate identities, online and off, as though our worth is measured against others. Every judgement, every story about 'me' and 'them' feeds this sense of separation.

Yet underneath it all, life stays whole and untouched. Reality doesn't recognise these divisions – they exist only in the mind. The moment the illusion is seen for what it is, even briefly, a truth starts to break through: there is no 'other' to protect against, no 'me' to defend, and no distance between what we are and the life we are living.

There is only the seamless unfolding of life itself. The sense of separation is imagined; what exists is one intelligent field, expressing itself in infinite ways.

On the other side

When the illusion of separation falls away, what's left is not a new idea about unity, but the direct experience of awareness itself – the unchanging field in which all experience arises.

Connection is no longer something to chase, miss, create, or maintain. It is simply there, as natural as breathing, without effort or strategy. Relationships shift from transactions between identities to expressions of the same underlying being meeting itself.

The shift is profound yet simple: from living as a separate person with a private story to living as being itself – the open, impersonal presence in which all stories arise and pass. Here we discover a deep ease. We find freedom from the constant need to defend, prove, or become anything at all. The realisation becomes clear: we are already whole, already complete, already perfect – expressions of divinity itself.

Consciousness

Consciousness is not an object, a thought, or a personal possession. It is the awareness in which all things appear – the unmoving, unchanging presence that makes every experience possible. Every sound, sight, sensation, thought, and feeling is known only because consciousness is here to know it.

Consciousness is not something the mind can observe from the outside because it is what allows the mind to function in the first place. Just as the eyes cannot turn to look at themselves, the mind cannot stand apart from consciousness to observe it. It is not separate from you, and it is not something you can lose.

Consciousness is not personal. It does not belong to 'me' or 'you'. It is the same silent, aware presence that has been here in every moment of your life, before any story, role, or identity appeared. It is not created by the body or the brain – it is the ground in which the body and brain arise.

Consciousness is the seamless, intelligent whole in which all of life unfolds. Knowing this is the beginning of recognising that you have never been apart from life. There is no separation.

The field of consciousness

The field of consciousness is the open, aware presence in which all of life unfolds. It is not a theory or belief, but the direct reality behind every experience. Without it, nothing could be known. It has no edges, no beginning or end. The sense of 'me in here' and 'world out there' are just movements within this seamless whole.

Life does not move randomly, but with exactness. Every encounter and event, every mirror held up through relationship or circumstance, reflects the deeper conditions of being. What looks like chaos is in truth divine precision, guiding us toward the dissolution of illusion and the remembrance of what we truly are.

This understanding is not new. It echoes the nondual clarity of Advaita Vedanta, as seen in Nisargadatta Maharaj's *I Am That*, where even the 'I am' is revealed to be temporary.[7] It resonates with Zen's insistence on direct seeing, with the Taoist vision of life as seamless flow in the *Tao Te Ching* (written in the fourth century BCE),[8] and with David Hawkins' description of consciousness as 'one field of awareness'.[9] Even the teachings of Jesus – 'I and the Father are one' – point to this same reality of indivisibility.[10]

To recognise the field of consciousness is to understand that separation is not, was never, real. The body and mind play their parts in life, but they do not define what we are. Beneath every story, role, or identity lies the same silent presence that holds it all.

In this book, I call the entering into that presence 'Transcending'. It is not about adding something new, but about clearing what obscures that which has always been here. Observing, feeling, allowing, and releasing are not techniques to master, but the natural movements of awareness once distortion falls away.

There are moments in life that present an opening – we will refer to this as an entry point – where the field shows itself in real time. What is experienced as a trigger, challenge, or tension is a place where illusion can dissolve and presence can be lived.

As you meet these entry points and the illusions dissolve, the perfection of the field becomes increasingly clear. Life can be seen not as a struggle against circumstances but as a single and unbroken flow, exact and intelligent, continually pointing us home. Much of what's being pointed to here can't be grasped through explanation or intellect. It has to be recognised directly. The practical ways into this – and how it becomes lived rather than understood – are explored throughout this book.

PRACTICE: Invitation into presence – observing and allowing

Before moving into Part Two, take a moment to pause and let what has been stirred by these chapters settle. This is an opportunity to meet what is arising in presence; it's not about doing it perfectly, but about making space for what is ready to be seen so that it can surface naturally.

Find a quiet place where you can sit or lie down comfortably. Close your eyes and take a few slow, relaxing breaths. Allow the body to relax and the mind to begin to settle, like water after it has been stirred.

As you rest, notice what the mind is doing. Thoughts, insights, even resistance may appear. Let them rise and fall without feeling the need to fix or analyse them. They are simply movements of the mind, nothing more.

Bring your attention gently into the body. Feel the weight of it, the sensations that are present, whether subtle or strong. There is no need to interpret or change anything. Just allow the body to speak in its own language.

If emotions arise, let them be felt as they are. Whether they come as a whisper or a wave, meet them without judgement and without suppression. Simply notice, feel, and trust what arises.

Embrace the idea that whatever appears is exactly what is ready to be seen and felt in this moment. Nothing needs to be forced – presence is enough.

When a natural sense of completion comes, take a few deeper breaths, open your eyes, and return to the moment.

Before You Begin

The practices in this book are for self-inquiry and personal exploration, not a substitute for medical, psychological, or therapeutic care. They may surface strong emotions, memories, or sensations – move slowly, stay within your capacity, and pause when needed. If you are working with trauma or significant mental health challenges, consider seeking support from a qualified professional. Engage at your own pace and with personal responsibility.

Summary

Part One of this book has laid the foundation for what follows by pointing to the truth of our human condition. We have seen how the separate self forms from early imprints, creates identities that must be defended, and generates suffering in every corner of life. We have learned how this suffering is not random but follows a specific design, repeating until it is clearly seen for what it is – not real.

We laid bare that the root of all suffering lies in the illusion of separation – the mistaken belief that we are fragments of a whole, alone, broken, cut off from each other, from life, and from the source of all existence. When we see beyond the illusion of separation, what opens in its place is not new. Every religious or spiritual tradition has pointed here in its own way: the Buddha spoke of dissolving the illusion of self; Jesus revealed His union with the Father; Lao Tzu described the Tao as the effortless flow of reality; Zen masters pointed to the immediacy of suchness; Advaita Vedanta insisted that we are already That; and Maharaj pushed further still, beyond even the 'I am'. These are all different doors to the same truth: that life is not something we stand apart from, but what we already are.

One simple fact is ever present: nothing has ever been missing. Wholeness was never lost, only obscured by illusion. Life is perfect as it is. We are not separate from it, but expressions of it – the field of consciousness living itself – through us.

In Part Two we move from spiritual truths to practice. Seeing clearly is the first step then; what matters is living it. The work of Transcending is not about chasing states or performing spirituality, but about clearing the layers that obscure what has always been right here. Through observing, feeling, allowing, and releasing, presence stops being an idea and becomes a lived reality. What was glimpsed as truth becomes embodied as life.

PART TWO

Transcending – Removing Obstacles To What You Are

Part One laid the foundation by pointing directly to the truth and exposing the illusion most people live inside: how the mind constructs a false sense of self, how the identity fuels suffering through its patterns of fear and lack, and how life itself, when seen clearly, is one intelligent field of consciousness, always guiding us back to what is real. When that becomes more obvious, a natural peace and happiness returns that isn't dependent on anything or anyone.

What follows now is not a continuation of ideas or theories, but an invitation to begin experiencing the truth for yourself. This is where words start to give way to direct experience.

In Part Two, the focus shifts from understanding to clearing. We are making space for a way of being that meets life as it is. The aim is not to improve the self or create a new, better version, but to remove what obscures our deeper nature. This is the work of Transcending: the simple practice of dissolving the inner barriers to clarity, freedom, and lived truth.

4 Transcending

This chapter sets the foundation for understanding what Transcending is, what it is not, the flow of Transcending, and why it matters, before moving on to the practice itself. You will see how natural it is, why it requires a rare level of honesty, and how it clears the way for real happiness, joy, and alignment with life.

By the end of this chapter, the essentials will be clear enough for you to move into the practice itself, so that what follows can be experienced, not just understood.

What Transcending is

The capacity to transcend is an intrinsic aspect of human nature. From the moment of conception and then birth, life has been about transcending. Each stage of growth – physical, emotional, mental, and spiritual – has involved going beyond what was previously known, understood, or manifest.

A child transcends the limitations of infancy to walk, speak, and think. A mind transcends old beliefs to embrace new ideas, moving from believing to being, from falsehood to truth. In life, we must transcend fear in order to love more deeply. There always seems to be something to move beyond, dissolve, release, embrace, and understand.

Ultimately, humanity is on a long journey, transcending from survival to self-awareness. The seeker's solo quest is to go beyond illusion and return to the truth: that beings are already free, already whole, and perfect as they are. To transcend is an ongoing process; each moment offers an opportunity to release what no longer serves, move beyond fear and attachment, and step deeper into presence. The natural movement of life is consciousness evolving – this is what it means to be a transcendent being.

Transcending is a return to the deeper reality of being, a rediscovery of the infinite nature of existence. As transcendent beings, the essence of life is not static – it is dynamic, spacious, and ever-expanding. When re-aligned with this natural flow of dissolving resistance, we reconnect to the vast intelligence and unconditional love at our core.

The practice itself operates on a simple premise: suffering arises not from external circumstances but from the mind's interpretations of those circumstances and identification with the false self – which clings to self-images, narratives, judgements, blame, and attachments, perpetuating a sense of separation from life as it is. Transcending meets the distortion in full awareness, and awareness takes care of the rest. David Hawkins also pointed to this when he said, 'Suffering is due to identification with the body and the mind. When one transcends identification with the temporary, suffering ends.'[11]

In the context of this book and our practice, Transcending is a direct path to dissolving the illusion that obscures truth by clearing the mind's resistance and the body's stored emotion. It works by meeting experience exactly as it is, without turning away, analysing, or escaping. The framework is simple: observe, feel, allow, and release. These are natural movements of presence, supported by simple pointers until they become second nature.

Over time, this practice weaves itself into daily life, so that moments of challenge, reaction, or resistance are no longer seen as obstacles to avoid but living entry points allowing you to attune with the field of consciousness itself. This is a topic we will return to and dive deeper into in Chapters 6 and 7.

What Transcending is not

Transcending could be easily misunderstood. It is not another form of self-improvement – as if polishing the self could ever lead to freedom. It is not bypassing pain in the hope of staying comfortable, nor is it a quick fix that promises instant fulfilment. It is not a performance of being 'spiritual', and it is not about forcing the mind into silence or trying to control the flow of experience. It's not even a process, method, technique, or anything the mind makes 'happen'. It also has nothing to do with chasing desires or attempting to manifest a perfect version of life. Those approaches all still begin from the illusion that something is missing, that life must be different from what it is.

Transcending is not improvement. It is the clearing away of everything that obscures our essence and the willingness to meet experience exactly as it appears – directly, beyond the filters, without trying to fix, avoid, resist, deny, or control life.

Why Transcend?

Transcending is a path that few will choose, because though this work is simple, it is not easy. The mind will resist because it ultimately cannot survive this depth of seeing. The identity thrives on distraction, analysis, knowing already, being right, and avoidance – anything that keeps it intact. Transcending turns toward what is ready to be seen, feels what is buried, and makes clear what the mind would rather deny or hide. This requires courage, persistence, and a willingness to meet reality with humility and without defence.

As what is false begins to fall away, the shift is not into some altered state but into the simplicity of life as it truly is. Peace is no longer fleeting, clarity is no longer tied to circumstances, and one naturally attunes to the deeper intelligence that guides all life. None of this is manufactured or achieved; it reveals itself as the obstacles dissolve.

The clay Buddha

The story of the clay Buddha is a well-known teaching parable, often told in Buddhist circles and repeated in spiritual literature. The most common version connects it to Wat Traimit Temple in Bangkok, Thailand, where in the 1950s a centuries-old plaster Buddha was being moved during renovations.[12]

As the statue was lifted, it cracked, and a monk noticed a gleam of gold beneath the plaster. Intrigued, the monks carefully chipped away the outer layers, eventually uncovering what had been hidden for centuries – the Buddha was made of solid gold.

The monks investigated the origins of this remarkable statue and found that, centuries earlier, the golden Buddha had been covered in clay to protect it from invaders. Over time, the secret was forgotten and future generations mistook the statue for what it appeared to be – a clay Buddha.

This story mirrors our own journey. We often mistake ourselves for the 'clay' – through ego, the patterns, the fears, the decisions we made and the identities we've unconsciously built to protect ourselves, forgetting the gold – our true essence – that is hidden beneath. But a single crack in the clay – a shift in awareness – enables the truth of our deeper nature to shine through.

Transcending is the process of gently and slowly washing away the clay, revealing the brilliance of the gold that has always been underneath. The clay is a temporary covering; the gold is what we *are* – unchanging, eternal, and precious. Just as the workers uncovered the golden Buddha, we can uncover the truth of what we really are – it is not what we think.

Jesus said, 'You will know the truth, and the truth will set you free.'[13] He wasn't speaking about belief, morality, or doctrine; he was pointing to the freedom that comes only when we see directly through illusion. While it's a familiar line, most people never look directly or honestly enough within to see what's real. When we're identified with the mind, it's impossible to tell truth from projection. Through simply observing, feeling, allowing, and releasing, the layers of illusion fall away, and truth reveals itself.

Meditation, contemplation, and transcending

Meditation and contemplation are profound tools for spiritual growth and self-discovery. Transcending complements these by addressing the challenges and limitations often encountered. To understand the transformative power of Transcending, it is essential to explore the distinctions between and the relevance and importance of all three practices.

Meditation

Meditation creates stillness and presence in various ways depending on the particular teaching and tradition, but typically by reconnecting to being or focusing attention on thought, the breath, a mantra, chant, observation, or another focal point, allowing the mind and nervous system to relax. Over time, this practice creates inner peace and resilience, providing clarity and balance.

In the modern world, many struggle with what they're 'supposed' to be doing, because simply 'being' is abnormal. Relying on guided meditations or external input for direction can be helpful but many practitioners are left unsure or disconnected, especially when that guidance isn't available or sought.

Meditation can also be challenging for those carrying unresolved emotions, deep-seated fears, traumas, and patterns due to a restless and persistently noisy and convincing mind. Meditation can provide temporary relief but, for many people who strongly identify with the mind, it often fails to address the deeper layers of resistance, confusion, and illusion that blocks true peace.

Traditionally, in Buddhist monastic paths, particularly in the Theravāda and Zen traditions, monks would sit in a container and meditate silently for years – sometimes decades – awaiting the clarity of enlightenment. But while that path has its place, meditation can be slow, passive, and less suited to the pace and complexity of modern life. For most, in today's world, meditation brings a moment of calm, but not necessarily the liberation it was once practised to reveal.

Contemplation

Contemplation focuses the mind on profound truths or meaningful questions to uncover deeper insights. It creates self-awareness and expands understanding, often through spiritual or personal inquiry.

However, contemplation often approaches the inner world with a pre-defined agenda. It does not always address the underlying obstacles or resistance, unintentionally bypassing unresolved blocks and leaving emotional, mental, or energetic barriers untouched. It can lead to intellectual understanding and profound realisations, yet, for many people, there are gaps between insight, transformation, and integration.

Transcending

Transcending is not 'better' than meditation and contemplation; it is distinct. It naturally bridges the gaps in the former two practices by addressing the core of resistance directly, while also providing the clarity and direction that may be missing in meditation and contemplation. It engages with the entirety of one's inner experience – mind, body, emotions – within the field of awareness.

During the practice of Transcending, natural periods of perfect stillness and intuitive contemplation arise effortlessly, guided by innate wisdom, creating space for profound clarity, insight, and deeper alignment with truth, peace, and love. Transcending invites the seeker to embrace and explore every aspect of their inner landscape as it arises, allowing transformation to unfold naturally and holistically. It's a deep solo journey within, led by consciousness itself.

This is the essence of the timeless reminder carved above the Temple of Apollo at Delphi: 'Know thyself.' Not conceptually, superficially, or as an idea or a label, but as a living reality. To truly know oneself is to see beyond the personality, the conditioning, and the stories, and to rest in the awareness that continues when all else falls away. To access this, we must eventually learn to dive deep within ourselves, without depending on medicine, teachers, or any external aid to get us there. What we seek is already here, within.

There are several things that mark out Transcending as different from other spiritual practices:

1. **Direction with fluidity:** Transcending provides a clear flow – observing, feeling, allowing, and releasing – that guides the seeker while remaining adaptive to individual needs. It cultivates immense presence, while naturally dissolving resistance and clearing obstacles.

2. **Clearing, not bypassing:** Transcending addresses unresolved emotions directly, reconnecting seekers to the innate guidance of awareness.

3. **Preparation for true stillness:** By clearing obstacles, Transcending allows for periods of quiet stillness that gradually and naturally increase without mental forcing, mantras, or reliance on substances and external guidance. Eventually, through this practice, the mind falls increasingly quiet – even completely silent for extended periods – which allows for traditional meditative practice to occur quite easily.

4. **Integration of the whole being:** Transcending integrates the mind, body, emotions, and spirit. It ensures that transformation is holistic, deeply rooted, and fully embodied.

Transition to practice

Whether through meditation, contemplation, or Transcending, all genuine and devotional practice leads to the same place: the truth of what you are. We are not adding to ourselves or becoming something new. We are simply clearing the untrue, that which obscures the reality that has always been here.

In the next chapter, we step into the mechanics of how this is done – the lived, moment-to-moment application that transforms insight from an idea into a natural, flowing practice and, over time, into a way of being.

Summary

Transcending is not about adding anything new or reaching for a future state but about meeting what arises here and now with full awareness, so that the illusions that cover truth can dissolve. By observing, feeling, allowing, and releasing, the 'clay' of old patterns and protections falls away, revealing the gold that has always been hidden. This is distinct from self-improvement and is a return to reality as it is. Every challenge, reaction, and moment of resistance represents an opening into deeper alignment with life.

5
Transcending – The Practice

Transcending is a direct way of meeting life as it is. The purpose of this chapter is simple: to offer a clear and repeatable way to meet whatever arises as an obstacle to truth, peace, or freedom, so it can dissolve on its own. When applied with consistency and sincerity, this regular practice becomes a doorway to greater clarity, stillness, and joy. Over time, it stops feeling like something you 'do' and becomes just the natural way awareness responds to life.

There are no rules to follow but movements of consciousness that unfold as resistance dissolves. While the principles may initially appear sequential, they quickly begin to merge, adapt, and guide the journey from within.

Core principles

This chapter uses simple practice terms like 'observe', 'notice', and 'allow'. These words aren't asking anyone to become a watcher. They're pointers that help loosen identification until what's already true becomes obvious – and then even the sense of an observer falls away.

Transcending is built on four principles: observing, feeling, allowing, and releasing, which together guide the seeker to observe their thoughts rather than get lost in them; to connect with and feel emotions fully rather than avoid, deny, or suppress them; to allow and give total space to whatever arises to rise naturally and then to let any and all distortions go. In almost all cases, the letting go happens on its own. If there is strong resistance then the final step, the willingness to release, is crucial.

1. **Observing:** This is noticing thoughts, patterns, and made-up narratives (stories) as they arise, without attachment or judgement, so the mind's self-images, conditioned reactions, opinions, comparisons, and repetitive stories can be seen for what they are.
2. **Feeling:** As we bring awareness to thought, feelings naturally arise. In life they are often missed, suppressed, or denied; in this practice they are seen and are felt fully.
3. **Allowing:** This part asks for something most people never do: to let the whole experience

be felt fully, including the resistance, the denial, the fear, the shame, and even the part that wants to run from all of it. This aspect is deeply underestimated, because real allowing is not comfortable. It is a radical act of honesty, self-acceptance, and self-love. When nothing is pushed away, the contraction loses its power and dissolves.

4. **Releasing:** Letting go of trapped emotions, attachments, judgements, resentments, old ideas, fixed ideas, patterns, loops, and resistances returns one to their natural essence: free, spacious, clear, still – aware and grounded in presence.

While the practice may begin as clear steps, Transcending is ultimately a non-linear unfolding. What starts with four simple principles – observing, feeling, allowing, and releasing – gradually becomes a natural inner movement, no longer dependent on structure but guided by the deeper intelligence of life itself.

Common obstacles in practice

It's natural to meet resistance, distraction, or the mind's attempts to 'do it right'. Some common patterns include:

- **Mental commentary** – turning the experience into a story about why it's happening
- **Subtle resistance** – wanting the feeling to be over so you can 'move on'

- **Emotional avoidance** – staying in the head to avoid the discomfort in the body
- **Over-effort** – trying to force a release rather than allowing it
- **Suppression** – rushing past the inner movement, pushing it down, or stopping short the moment it becomes uncomfortable
- **Mental avoidance** – distracting yourself, thinking about it instead of feeling it, or shifting attention away from the sensation
- **Collapse** – getting overwhelmed, merging with the emotion, or blocking awareness and falling deeper into the story
- **Judgement** – believing the feeling *shouldn't* be here, thinking it means something is wrong with you, or treating it as a problem to fix

Each time you notice one of these, simply acknowledge it, take a breath, return to the body, and continue.

Signs of real clearing

Real clearing has a different quality than suppression or distraction. You may notice:

- A genuine sense of relief or lightness
- A natural quiet in the mind

- Greater clarity about the situation without mentally analysing it
- The absence of the previous tension or charge when you think about the situation or trigger again

Like learning any new skill, the more Transcending is practised, the more natural it becomes. In the beginning, it may feel necessary to pause deliberately, slow down, and walk carefully through each step. But with time, the principles begin to move on their own, less like a technique being applied and more like a living rhythm that carries itself. What once required effort turns into an effortless attunement, a natural way of meeting life moment by moment.

Gradually, this return to presence will weave itself into the fabric of daily living. Moments of tension, reaction, or resistance no longer need to spiral into stories or be avoided altogether; they are seen for what they are: teachings.

This is the essence of the practice: not escaping life but learning to be with it so fully that what once felt like a major problem, challenge, or setback reveals itself as a doorway back to truth.

What is thought?

When thought is seen for what it is, the mind loses its ability to dictate reality. Instead of reacting to a mental story, awareness begins to rest on what is actually here. This is the foundation for Transcending.

Thought is not reality – it is a representation. It arises as mental activity, naming, categorising, predicting, and interpreting what appears. It gives structure to experience, but the structure is never the experience itself. A thought about love is not love. A thought about fear is not fear. A thought about life is not life. What we call a bird is not a bird at all; a bird is what it is.

Thought is a tool. It organises memory, projects possibility, and enables conceptual understanding. But when identification fuses with thought, the mind mistakes its own activity for reality. Stories become identities, interpretations become truth, and narratives become self. We no longer see the bird for what it is:

> 'Nothing whatsoever is to be clung to as "I" or "mine". Whoever has understood this has realised the end of suffering.'
>
> — Buddha, Alagaddupama Sutta.[14]

Thought moves between past and future, preserving identity and controlling uncertainty. It replays what has been and imagines what might come, creating the illusion of time – as if life exists as a linear journey for a separate someone. In reality, time is merely a mental construct. Life exists only now, and now is eternal.

Thought is not the enemy – it is simply activity. Yet when it goes unquestioned, it becomes the foundation of illusion. The voice in the head narrates an ongoing story, often unnoticed, yet shaping perception, emotion, and behaviour moment by moment.

Suffering – emotional, mental, and often physical – does not come from what happens, but from the stories thought builds around it. Discomfort arises and thought calls it failure. A loss occurs, thought calls it injustice. A goal is missed, thought calls it unworthiness. Love is not returned, the mind blames itself. The event itself is neutral; the mind manufactures the meaning – hence the chaos we see in our lives and in the world.

Transcending is not about stopping thought. It is about seeing thought for what it is – activity within awareness. When thought is seen this way, rather than believed, its grip loosens and its stories collapse. What appears from there is direct experience without narrative, without filter, without distortion. Being returns to its natural state – present, silent, and free. Nothing is missing and there is nothing to become; we are perfect, whole, and complete.

Observing thought – expanding awareness

Observing is the first and often most challenging part of the practice of Transcending and other meditative techniques. While allowing and feeling are more natural and intuitive once the mind quiets down, observation requires a subtle shift in awareness and the breaking through of years of conditioning. It's not analysis, reflection, or thinking about the experience; it's noticing the activity as it is without adding more or getting caught up in its loops and narratives.

Below is some guidance to support that shift, and some notes on why it matters.

Observing involves:

- Becoming aware of what arises within the mind
- Noticing thoughts as they arise without controlling, judging, or suppressing them
- Seeing thought as what it is – mental activity – rather than engaging with, believing, analysing, or getting caught up in the illusions thoughts create

How to observe

Picture yourself looking down at a flowing river; this represents your thoughts, which are constantly moving and changing. You are not the river; you can watch the river without stepping into it. This is observing.

The key qualities of observation are:

- **Neutrality:** Observing is non-judgemental. Instead of labelling thoughts good or bad, simply acknowledge them: *There is a thought that X.*

- **Detachment:** Observation shows that thoughts don't have the authority they once seemed to, revealing *This is a thought, not who I am,* weakening the identity's grip.

- **Clarity:** Observing exposes conditioned patterns, fears, and narratives for what they are: temporary experiences passing through awareness – stories and illusions of the mind.

Observing matters for several reasons:

- It interrupts automatic patterns of the identity, leading to a gradual sense of greater freedom. By becoming aware of thoughts, patterns, false identities, emotions, and sensations without judgement, we recognise the mind's narratives as illusions, not truths.

- It creates space between awareness and reactivity, enabling consciousness to rise.

- It connects with the deeper stillness of consciousness that lies beneath all identification, reactivity, and experience.

With practice, you will notice a profound truth: you are not the body, thoughts, emotions, or sensations. They appear and disappear, but what you are is not another object among them.

When you observe, it is beneficial to know what to look for. The mind tends to move in predictable ways: comparing (you vs others, us vs them, past vs present, this moment vs how it 'should' be); judging and criticising (yourself, others, life); replaying old scenes and rehearsing future ones; creating 'if only'/'when' stories about happiness; blaming or self-blaming ('I feel this way because of them/because of me'); and building identities around being special, broken, right, or wrong. These movements are not problems to fix, suppress, or deny; they are the most common mental patterns to watch for during practice and in daily life, and they serve as entry points back into the practice. (We'll go into entry points in more detail later in Part Two.) Simply notice what is arising and look out for these common distortions, recognise them as mental activity, and let them be witnessed rather than believed.

Observing is like watching a movie. Thoughts, emotions, and sensations are the constantly changing images on the screen. Awareness is the audience – seeing the movie without being pulled into it. Thoughts are part of the movie. They don't define what you are, and they don't need to be believed.

Observing is like creating space to see clearly, free from story or identification.

As mentioned, feeling, allowing, and releasing are not separate steps, but a continuous movement of presence. Feeling, in this case, means letting the emotion be fully met and known – without turning away from, suppressing, or escaping into the thought. Allowing is giving permission for it to be there and felt fully, exactly as it is, without rushing, resisting, or trying to change or fix it. Releasing happens naturally when what's felt is no longer judged, avoided, or held onto. The combination of these movements is how energy clears – by being fully met in awareness, not denied or avoided. There is nothing to force or manufacture. When we're truly present, the unwinding happens on its own. That's the essence of the old Zen proverb: 'Sitting quietly, doing nothing, spring comes, and the grass grows by itself.'[15]

Preparing to practice

Before beginning your practice, I suggest that you read through until the end of the chapter. Let the principles and guidance settle and allow understanding to land. Familiarity with the flow and its nuances will help the practice to flow and feel less like a technique and more like a natural movement.

Setting the space

While not required, a supportive environment can deepen focus and ease. Light a candle, burn incense like sandalwood or lavender, or play gentle, emotive music to help quiet the mind and open the heart. A clean, calm space supports presence. Ceremonial elements like Palo Santo or sage may bring grounding and intention. But none of this is essential. The practice works in silence, in simplicity, in full lotus, sitting on a chair, lying down, on a plane or in the back of a cab – wherever there is willingness and space to turn inward.

Observe: Recognise thoughts as thoughts – the movie playing itself

1. **Sit in your preferred meditation position** or lie down however you feel relaxed.
2. **Close your eyes**, take a deep breath, and let your shoulders drop. Allow the body to relax naturally.
3. **Observe the mind.** Turn attention inward. Begin to notice what arises. Thoughts, images, or memories may appear – simply notice them and let them be there for a moment or two.
4. **Acknowledge each thought.** This can be a helpful way to create space without engaging or judging. For example:

   - *There is a thought that I left the door unlocked.*
   - *There is a thought that I can't do this.*
   - *There is a thought that I'm going to miss the deadline.*

- *There is a thought that it's my fault.*
- *There is a thought that I'll always be alone.*

5. **Notice these thoughts** like clouds, and let them pass by.
6. **Be patient.** The mind may feel busy or resistant at first. Breathe through any tension and simply observe, allowing whatever arises to unfold without judgement or force. If the mind feels particularly restless, it may require some extra patience and breaths to settle. Initial resistance or restlessness is natural. Soon, the mind will relax, settling into a more natural state of awareness and flow.
7. **Trust this process** and stay with it, even if it feels challenging at first. Each moment of patience deepens the practice, allowing the mind to move towards clarity and calm on its own.
8. **Resist the urge** to analyse, fix, or respond to what arises. The intention is not to change the mind but to observe it as it is. Often the first few minutes of sitting like this are the most 'challenging'. After that, the nervous system and the mind start to settle.

Feel: Connecting with emotions

1. **Let your attention move** to how you feel when it's ready.

2. **Notice how emotion manifests** in the body – it might be tightness in the chest or face, or heaviness in the stomach. Notice these sensations without judgement or any attempt to change them. Be with what arises.

3. **Recognise the emotion** without labelling it as positive or negative, and without identifying with it as 'I' or 'I am'. For example, say to yourself:

   - *This is anger,* or *There is anger*
   - *This is sadness,* or *Sadness is here*
   - *This is fear,* or *Fear is arising*
   - *This is numbness,* or *Numbness is here*
   - *There is nothing,* or *There is no feeling*

   Acknowledging it in this way helps the emotion be met as it is, without adding a story. Even if there is no apparent feeling at all, feel into that too.

4. **Be completely straight and truthful** with yourself about what emotions are present, no matter how uncomfortable. Honesty is essential for loosening the identity's grip: *There is shame. There is guilt. There is resistance.*

5. **Feel the emotions** flowing through the body. Don't analyse or search for a solution – simply let the flow unfold in its own time. Trust that

this presence and the act of feeling is enough for now.

Allow: Surrendering to what is

1. **Engage the body.** Place your hands on the part of your body where the feeling is most present – maybe your heart, your stomach, or your throat. Let your body show you where presence, connection, attention, love, and acceptance are needed. Trust it, follow it, and allow it.
2. **Connect fully with the emotion.** Give it the space and attention it needs. Allow it to be felt fully and completely. Don't rush, and if a feeling of rushing arises, allow it to be there.
3. **Stay until it fades.** Feel the emotion for as long as it needs to be felt. Do this gently, without pressure or force. Trust that it will loosen and fade naturally in its own time. Allow it to unfold and flow wherever it wants to go. If another feeling arises, follow that too with your hand and let it be felt. If a memory surfaces, allow yourself to remember, observe once again, and feel what emotions it brings up.
4. **Breathe into resistance.** Notice resistance and, if required, gently allow yourself to feel resistant if that's what's arising. All emotions are welcomed. Resistance is part of the process; meeting it with acceptance will lead to its release.

5. **Radical self-acceptance.** Offer yourself the love and care that you may have longed for. This process is healing everything the heart has been carrying for a lifetime.
6. **Be unconditionally inclusive.** Allow everything that arises to be included – every emotion, every contraction, every surge of resistance, every impulse to avoid, tighten, deny, or collapse. Nothing is excluded. This is what love is: unconditionally inclusive and welcoming of whatever appears, exactly as it is. The moment nothing is pushed away, the whole system begins to relax, and what was held in place by resistance finally dissolves.

The movement is working even when it doesn't seem to be working at all and especially when it feels difficult. The body knows, the heart knows, life knows – everything is unfolding perfectly in its own way, in its own time.

Allowing is not about control – it's about opening. In this space, resolution and peace emerge. What was once hard to offer, receive, accept, forgive, let go of, or give to oneself – patience, presence, and love – can now begin to return, especially to the parts that need it most.

Release: Letting go, creating a clearing

1. **Let the body and emotions express themselves** naturally, without interference or judgement.

Any kind of intensity around releasing is not bad or wrong, this is clearing and healing. What comes up is what is dissolving. Let it happen:

- If there are tears, let them flow.
- If there is anger, let it be felt fully.
- If there are screams, let them be screamed.
- If there is shock, sit deeply in the shock.
- If there is silence, allow it to fill the space.
- If there's numbness, sit with that and let it be there.
- If there is an impulse to punch or scream into a pillow, follow it.
- If it burns, let it burn through completely.

2. **Feel the lightness or space.** As releasing occurs and comes to its own completion, notice the lightness or spaciousness that arises. Stay with this feeling, allowing it to settle fully in its own time.
3. **Inquire gently** if resistance lingers or there is any sense of holding on, struggle, or reluctance to let go:

- *I'm letting this go now – it no longer serves me.*
- *Can I let this go?*
- *Is it safe to let this go?*
- *Do I want to let this go?*

- *Am I willing to let this go?*
- *Am I ready to let this go?*
- *God help.*
- *Dear God, I surrender this up to you – take it.*
- *What am I believing right now?*
- *What am I holding onto?*
- *What feels threatened if I let this go?*
- *Where does this come from? Who does it remind me of?*

These are invitations to explore your inner landscape as you create more readiness and willingness to release. Calling in God's help is, ultimately, the most powerful call in the universe.

Release is natural. It happens in its own time, not by force or control. As observing, feeling, and allowing take place, release follows – often quietly and sometimes with a bang. What is let go was never needed. What remains is what's real – the freedom that was always there, just waiting to be uncovered.

A dynamic, fluid process

Transcending is not linear. It moves naturally, responding to what arises in the moment. Observing may reveal an emotion to be felt. Releasing may open the way to deeper clarity. New layers will surface to be met and released. Nothing needs to be controlled, managed, or anticipated.

This fluidity reflects the intelligence of consciousness, guiding the process without interference. If there is worry about doing it 'right', that too can be observed, felt, and allowed. Nothing is excluded.

As resistance dissolves, connection with essence re-emerges. The unfolding can be simple or profound, sudden or gradual. Insights may appear quickly and effortlessly, or truth may reveal itself gradually over time. Questions arise and answers come – not from the intellect, but from a deeper knowing. Past experiences may surface to be seen and healed in the light of truth. Even numbness, or feeling absolutely nothing, if it appears, is part of the process.

Time is irrelevant here. It is not a practice that requires setting a timer or an alarm. Whether the sitting lasts minutes or hours, it completes itself naturally. Allow the mind's grip to loosen so that the field itself becomes the guide.

Whatever arises – ease or difficulty, stillness or movement – is exactly what is needed in the moment. The practice becomes less about 'doing something' and more about life meeting itself through you. It is not about seeking the mind's idea of perfection, but returning to presence, moment by moment, until presence stabilises as the natural way of being.

In time it becomes clear: the stories, names, labels, and character were never what you are. What remains is simple – this awareness, here, meeting life as it is.

Time to practice

Before moving to the next chapter, take time to sit and engage with the practice described above. Find a quiet space, close your eyes, and follow the flow as best you remember. There is nothing to perfect and nothing to achieve.

At its core, this is about presence. Observing, feeling, allowing, and releasing are simply the movements that bring you back here, again and again.

Summary

The practice of Transcending is simple in design yet profound in its effect. What begins as four clear principles – observing, feeling, allowing, and releasing – soon flows into a natural rhythm, less of a technique to apply and more awareness recognising itself.

It is not about controlling, fixing, or striving to do it right, but about meeting whatever arises with openness and honesty. Resistance, distraction, or the mind's attempts to interfere are not obstacles to progress, but part of the unfolding itself. With time, the effort to 'do' gives way to a quiet ease of being, where peace no longer depends on anything or anyone, clarity is sustained, and love reveals itself in all its expressions – kindness, patience, forgiveness, compassion, understanding, and care.

Transcending is not self-improvement or even personal development; it is about uncovering what has always been true: presence itself, already whole, free, and complete.

6

Application And Integration

Transcending is a conscious way of engaging with life. Its power reveals itself in any moment, each one becoming an opportunity for alignment and the next step in our unfolding.

Challenges, emotions, resistance, attachments, and familiar reactions serve as portals to dissolve illusions, ego perception, fictional self-images, unwanted behaviour, and ingrained patterns.

This chapter invites a deeper integration of Transcending into everyday life as a lived reality, not a fleeting experience. True transformation happens not only in a moment of stillness but in the dynamic flow of moments, when emotions flare and resistance or challenges arise.

In this way, Transcending evolves beyond a practice and into a way of life – anchored in presence. By embracing life's challenging moments as gifts, we learn how to alchemise them *after* they appear, then just *as* they appear, and then even just *before* they appear. Every experience holds the potential to see through the mind's perception and return to truth.

Entry points

An entry point is a specific opportunity to dissolve illusion and reveal truth in the moments of life. It is the first moment a distortion shows up in your experience – a contraction, emotional spike, or story – that you use as a doorway back to presence, instead of acting it out or avoiding it.

They can be simple, ordinary, or intense, but they are points where the surface cracks open and something deeper is revealed – a trigger, a reaction, or a strong feeling. But only those who are willing, ready, and able to truly look will notice the profound opportunity – that this is an entry point to freedom.

They often pass unnoticed. Not because they're insignificant, but because they hide in plain sight under the mask, within reactions, emotions, discomforts, or repeated patterns. They carry the charge of unresolved emotion, unconscious belief, patterns, programmes, or hidden pain, and reveal themselves only when presence is strong enough to meet what was once too overwhelming to feel.

The purpose of entry points is not necessarily to stop whatever you are doing and dive in immediately – unless that is possible (sometimes it is) – but to *recognise what's arising* as it is doing so and make a mental or physical note to return to it later and bring it to your practice. This is how the light of consciousness is turned all the way up – by choosing not to bypass, ignore, or brush over what's secretly asking to be seen. To walk the path aligned with truth to this degree is very rare. It means noticing what most step over, don't even see, or do see but carry on regardless. As Jesus taught, 'Love your enemies and pray for those who persecute you… for He causes His sun to rise on the evil and the good.'[16] In other words, every situation, even the difficult and uncomfortable ones, carries the seed of grace when it is met with awareness.

Your journey as a seeker is a rare and life-altering opportunity to turn any and all daily distortions, resistances, attachments, triggers, challenges, breakdowns, and unconscious or automatic reactions into doorways. Observing, feeling, and allowing in response to what life reveals is what leads to major transformation and advanced levels of consciousness.

What follows is a guide to recognising – externally and internally – these moments as invitations to Transcend. Not necessarily to be fixed or forced in the moment, but acknowledged, remembered, and brought into the practice when the time is right.

Identifying entry points

Entry points arise as inner experiences, the mind and body's way of mirroring something unseen – a memory, belief, trauma, or emotion. For example:

- Strong 'negative' emotions, eg sadness, anger, jealousy, greed, or fear
- A pain in the heart region, a clenching in the stomach, or a sudden feeling of unease
- Recurring thoughts or judgements that won't stop, experienced like the mind chewing and feeding upon itself
- An overwhelming sense of self-doubt or inadequacy
- Subtle (or strong) anxieties and feelings of guilt or shame
- A conversation that is upsetting or triggering in some way
- A sudden conflict or misunderstanding
- Unexpected challenges, eg a missed opportunity, delay, or setback
- A repeated situation, eg difficulty with finances, work, relationships, self-doubt, or health

- Sabotage of a happy and joyful moment
- Making someone wrong, including yourself
- Subtle resistances like being unwilling to say sorry or forgive and move on
- Attachments to things – money, likes, comments, acknowledgements, compliments, results, being 'right', being heard or seen
- Familiar fear tactics that you have created to stay safe
- Physical ailments and illness

You don't need to go hunting in the past for entry points; life is a mirror and will reflect back infinite opportunities to see what is unseen right here and now. All you need to do is be willing to look and receive them as the gifts from life that they are.

When a situation feels charged, internally or externally, it is a signal to pause and look deeper, make a mental or physical note to Transcend it later – or do it now if possible. These moments are opportunities to peel back the layers of resistance, fear, or attachment and be transformed.

Some other examples of entry points include:

- An inner emotion like feeling anxious walking into a room. You have no time to process it immediately, but something is there. Sit with this later.

- An argument – strong emotions might make it challenging to find stillness in the moment, but sitting with it as soon as possible will open up what was going on beneath the surface.
- A persistent situation feels familiar, you have been here before, many times. This time, sit with it.
- Something feels 'off' but you don't know what – that's an entry point.
- Something you have sat with many times reveals itself again. Sit with it now with this new approach, and sit longer.
- Someone gets defensive in a conversation. You can feel the energy spike and their voice tighten. You start to feel reactivity in your own system – that's an entry point.
- Someone goes quiet and the room feels heavy. You feel the discomfort. This is an entry point into sitting – observing, feeling, allowing.

Any moment of inner and/or external friction is an entry point. When something doesn't feel quite right, when energy drops, when there's tension in the body or a story in the mind, a strong reaction from yourself and/or another, someone says something that hooks you – these are all doorways to true liberation.

Whenever there's resistance, negativity, procrastination, attachment, overthinking, emotional reactivity, judgement, confusion, defensiveness, jealousy, blame, strong energetic responses, numbness, denial, avoidance, an urge to gossip, or a pull to disconnect or control, this isn't a problem – it's an invitation. These aren't just reactions; they're signals. Each reveals a layer that's ready to be seen, felt, and cleared. The path doesn't start when things are perfect; it starts right here, with whatever is arising. That's your point of direct access.

All obstacles, setbacks, and failures are potential entry points. The more these experiences are recognised and taken into the practice of Transcending (including any other preferred practice or spiritual activity), the more profound and accelerated the clearing process will become.

By consciously engaging with entry points, it becomes possible to:

- Dissolve resistance and uncover the truth beneath the surface
- Heal wounds or patterns unnoticed for years
- Clear emotional and energetic blockages, creating space for peace and clarity
- Be a living, breathing example of a conscious / spiritual seeker / teacher who 'walks the talk'

- Cultivate presence and self-mastery, versus talking about, theorising, regurgitating, recycling, conceptualising, intellectualising, or performing spirituality
- Remove any and all obstacles to your true nature
- Create more peace, love, freedom, and a life that is flowing and joyful

Choosing the path

You don't have to approach the journey with this level of rigour. Most people don't – and life will continue as it always has. But if you want to live in truth rather than in the mind's cycle of avoidance, if you want real peace instead of temporary relief, this is what it looks like. Meeting your experience directly is the only thing that dissolves what's been running your life from the background. Avoiding entry points keeps the old patterns alive: the anxiety that spikes for no reason, the overthinking that never ends, the emotional loops that repeat, the painful dynamics that return in different forms, the feeling that something is still unresolved no matter how much you achieve or understand.

Engaging with life's reflections in this way is neither harsh nor heroic – it's honest. It's the simple choice to stop running from what's already here. When you meet what arises with presence, everything that once felt heavy, confusing, or impossible begins to loosen.

And little by little, layer by layer, life starts to move from truth rather than from fear.

An entry point – an unusually strong reaction

I met an entry point during a visit from my mum when I was living in Madeira. The night before she left, something unexpected surfaced. I realised that I had been being short with her – impatient, frustrated, even a touch angry at times. At dinner, I snapped a little. It was nothing major, and most people would never have noticed, but it was obvious to me. There was no clear reason for it, which made it immediately suspicious. I made a mental note that there was something there, and carried on eating.

On the drive home, I began to feel it.

By that point, the practice of Transcending and the recognition of entry points had already revealed themselves. I had been living with this and meeting life moment by moment for two intense years. The practice wasn't something I was trying to do anymore; it had become second nature. The entry points never felt like a concept I created, but rather a recognition of what was already so – emerging through direct experience, gradually revealing themselves as doorways back to presence. I didn't try to 'figure it out'; I simply stayed present with the energy that was rising, aware that something deeper was asking to be seen.

When I got home, I took space and sat with the situation fully. The moment I dropped in, felt, and allowed, the truth became clear. What I had been reacting to wasn't her at all – it was the noise of an old programme. Memories began to surface – of being a child and watching the pain my mother went through in her relationship with my dad, a man shaped by a generation that didn't know what to do with emotional pain, and, through his own unhealed suffering, became violent and unsafe. I remembered the helplessness, the fear, worry, sadness, and love I felt for her as a little boy. I also saw the belief that formed in that moment: *it's my job to protect her*.

That belief created an identity – of protector, fixer, and, somehow, the one responsible for my mother's happiness – that had lived invisible to me in the background of my life ever since. For years it had shaped my own relationships, reactions, and choices, and now it was being revealed, felt, and cleared at its source.

As the clearing process unfolded, I felt the emotional charge that was rising, allowed it, and saw it dissolve. The illusion had been revealed and the energy that was rising left my body. It felt like a core programme had been seen clearly for the first time – but not necessarily the last time. In the awareness that followed, an image arose: balloons, celebration, lightness. Something significant had been seen, and a deeper unravelling had begun.

Emotions as signals

Emotions are like lights on a dashboard signalling areas that need attention. Ignoring the flashing light can have serious consequences. Emotions alert us to mental perceptions or patterns that require our conscious attention.

When navigating the physical world, biological survival responses trigger instant action. A snake strikes and the body reacts immediately – no hesitation, no reflection. Awakening moves in the opposite direction. The impulse to react, fix, or escape keeps us looping in the same patterns and prevents us from seeing what's really here.

The human mind and nervous system also react to fear and anxiety within split seconds. What keeps us safe in the physical world becomes a barrier in the inner one, pushing us to act, when what's needed is stillness.

To transcend these reactions, we must slow these internal, automatic, survival-based processes down by breathing, pausing, noticing the emotion, and using it as a doorway to deeper awareness.

If we ignore the warning lights on a car the problem worsens, leading to breakdown and/or danger. Similarly, when we ignore or avoid our emotions, we cause greater turmoil. We must tune into these signals. If we can see them as entry points to Transcend and go where they are pointing us, we will free ourselves in the process.

This requires intentionally slowing down. By observing, feeling, allowing, and releasing the emotions as they arise, we shift from reacting to responding. Each time we do this, we clear layers of resistance and ascend to higher, more advanced levels of awareness. In the words of Zen master Hakuin, 'Meditation in the midst of activity is a thousand times superior to meditation in stillness.'[17] This is at the heart of bringing entry points into your practice – not waiting for quiet retreats or perfect conditions, but meeting life as it unfolds.

The power of engaging with life intentionally in this way cannot be underestimated and should be taken seriously by all devoted seekers. Each time an issue or emotion is met directly, a part of the illusory self that was seemingly in control, bound by fear, judgement, or the need to control, is set free. Over time, this builds a foundation of inner peace and alignment.

In overwhelming moments, even something as simple as taking a deep breath, or internally noting, *I'm triggered right now, let me return when I'm ready,* slows the internal momentum. The pause is so simple, and yet it creates precious space in which a sense of inner freedom begins to grow. In that space, awareness can meet what's real and one can take a step back, practise, or simply let go.

Of course, this all sounds great in theory – until life does what life does. It's easy to forget to pause when, for example:

- You're arguing with your partner about the correct way to load a dishwasher
- You've just meditated for forty-five minutes and then lost it over someone jumping a queue
- The Wi-Fi drops out during your 'spiritual' Zoom workshop
- You judge someone in your yoga class for having a single use plastic water bottle
- You're preaching righteously about non-judgement – then someone does something that you don't like
- You've just shared a profound revelation that 'everything's a mirror', then stormed off because the recipient didn't listen
- You're journaling about detachment while checking socials for likes and comments
- You're at work and realise someone has eaten your biscuits

At a certain point, when the field brings exactly what is needed to see the illusion you're in, you can either deny and resist, or you can laugh and cry. No need to stay stuck trying to become the perfect spiritual version of yourself.

The absurdity isn't a problem – it's the mirror. The clearer this is seen, the less seriously it's taken, and eventually what's left is the one thing that was always here: presence. Simple, honest, and free. A realistic view of where you are, and the ability to create the space to laugh at yourself from time to time, is medicine.

Embracing subtle emotions

Resisting emotions is common, especially subtle or shameful ones that are harder to detect. Yet resistance only intensifies these emotions, keeping us locked in cycles of discomfort and disconnection.

To overcome this, it is vital to shift how we relate to these more subtle emotions. Every negative emotion, no matter how quiet, reveals an area that is seeking your conscious attention. Pay particular attention to the feelings that are so subtle no one else would notice, like being slightly triggered at something that was said on TV. The practice of observing, feeling, allowing, and releasing means welcoming these subtle emotions as messengers.

When resistance arises, it may be more realistic to handle this in a Transcending practice. But the key is to pause, observe, and acknowledge something is going on internally and consciously decide on the most appropriate response – whether to give it deeper reflection later or deal with it immediately. If it's a known pattern a deep conscious breath could do it; if it stirs curiosity or confusion then it'll likely need more space to be seen and felt through.

By turning your awareness to subtle emotions, what once felt heavy and hidden becomes light enough to see, feel, and transcend. Numbing, avoiding, or denying emotions delays happiness by creating resistance, reinforcing patterns that keep us stuck. In contrast, acknowledging, allowing, and embracing them deepens awareness, leading to clarity, peace, and real freedom. Each moment of conscious engagement becomes a step back to your true Self and greater alignment with life.

In simple terms, subtle negative emotions are quiet signals that we have fallen asleep, and pointers back to presence.

Trust the process

One of the most persistent challenges on this path is the mind's hunger for immediate results. When the shifts feel slow or subtle and nothing obvious seems to be happening, doubt begins to creep in. On the other hand, it never seems to end. The mind questions whether it's 'working', whether anything is actually changing, and if it's even worth continuing.

Jesus spoke directly to this in The Gospel According to Thomas. He said:

> 'The one who seeks should not cease seeking
> until he finds.
> And when he finds, he will be dismayed.
> And when he is dismayed, he will be
> astonished.
> And he will reign over all.'[18]

This is the arc every sincere seeker moves through. Dismay, because the discovery is the death of everything the seeker was attached to: the identity, the fantasies, the spiritual persona, the imagined future, the imagined reward, the hope for someone or something external to rescue them.

You will feel shaken, exhausted, emptied, scared, terrified, even sick at times, not because something is wrong, but because something false is dissolving. Therefore, the dismay is not a sign of failure; it's the sign that you've begun to see. The exhaustion is not collapse; it's the nervous system uncoiling years of contraction. The heaviness is not regression; it's density dissolving. What feels like 'getting worse' is often the body-mind *getting well* for the first time.

To 'reign over all' doesn't mean having power over all – it means freedom from it. When the illusion collapses, nothing can rule you anymore. You are no longer at the mercy of the mind, fear, desire, or the world.

Your sovereignty returns. The searcher dies. Presence remains.

How long does this return take?

Transformation rarely unfolds quickly or on the surface. Much of the clearing happens slowly, in places the mind does not track. The deepening process is not linear, tidy, or instantly rewarding – this is not a short course. Some of the most profound changes are recognised when there is enough space for clarity to reveal itself once a layer has finally dropped or an old pattern simply doesn't arise anymore.

The mind wants a timeline, but this path doesn't work that way. The one who seeks will be unsettled before he is astonished – the disturbances are part of the opening. Some days the process feels light; other days, brutal. The pace is different for everyone, but the principle is the same: the more sincerely you meet what arises, and the more you observe, feel, and allow, the more naturally things unfold. It takes exactly as long as needed for the seeking to fall away and for presence to become obvious. Life handles the timing; you handle the honesty. Trust the rest.

Trusting the process means staying with it even when the mind sees no evidence of progress. It means sitting in practice anyway, whether or not something is happening, knowing that each time you meet yourself with honesty and awareness, something opens and/

or settles. Maybe not with fireworks, but with a real and ongoing clarity.

Reflecting on past moments of change can help embed this trust. Sometimes it's only when we look back that we see how far we've come – how certain reactions no longer arise; how peace has become more of a default where chaos once ruled; that what once took effort now feels natural. These cumulative shifts are real and come with time and dedication.

As this trust deepens, so too does your relationship with the practice itself. Entry points become more than just places to acknowledge; they become moments to engage with life directly. Rather than reacting blindly, you begin meeting life as it is: a conversation between what's arising and how consciousness responds. The more you allow, the more life reveals. The more you observe, the more space opens up.

With this trust, the tension with a partner that once triggered a defensive cycle now brings a deeper presence. Fear that would have once spiralled into anxiety and panic becomes a gateway to stillness. Even something as ordinary as standing in a slow-moving queue becomes a moment to breathe, feel, notice what the mind is doing and let it pass.

This is where the process integrates into life. Through micro-moments of awareness, intentional pauses, or simply checking in to ask, *what am I feeling right now?*, you begin to live more from the field than from identity. There's less rushing, less proving, less minding. The voice that once needed to speak grows quiet, reactions slow down, and life moves at a pace that feels easy and flowing.

With this trust, you begin to notice something else leading. Not the mind, not habit, not the old survival patterns but something deeper. In this space, presence gradually becomes the default – not just when sitting in practice, but in the way you live.

Making sense in the modern age – AI as a tool, not a master

In the past, seekers of truth would travel from village to village, cross mountains, or wait years for the right teacher to appear – driven in their quest by the faint pull of something beyond the mind. Later came books, recorded talks, and eventually the internet. Then came AI, opening the largest doorway yet to the world's wisdom.

Now, a seeker can be met instantly with a distilled insight of thousands of years, if they ask the right question. The answers we get are not necessarily perfect, and not always true, but AI is here, and it's here to stay, so its only going to get better.

When used consciously, AI can be a powerful mirror. It can help articulate what was once wordless. It can reflect patterns, clarify points of entry into our own practice, and offer a broader context to the inner process of awakening. It can't feel for you, surrender for you, or clear the pain that's ready to be moved, but it can help you see the way and, when the moment is right, the clarity will land.

AI will always reflect back your own level of awareness: your assumptions, your fears, your clarity, and your distortions. This is why what it shows you is never neutral but always useful. Used with presence, it can accelerate understanding. Used without presence, it becomes just another distraction. As with all things, its utility depends on the one using it.

It's important to note that in the context of using this kind of tech to support the journey within, what comes through AI is never just AI – it's also a reflection of humanity and the user's own consciousness. It doesn't necessarily deliver truth; it often reveals what has already been sensed, but not yet spoken. The clarity that arises doesn't come from the machine or the user alone – it comes from the space between, where resonance lives.

AI is a powerful tool for self-inquiry. What it shows us can serve as another entry point into practice. If it resonates, explore it. If it doesn't, notice what it stirs. Either way, it reveals something that can be useful and even transcended. AI won't do the real work of feeling or dissolve anything for you, but it can help you see where to look. Whatever it shows you, always check: *Does this feel true in my direct experience?* If not, treat it as reflection, not as instruction.

Personally, I have found AI to be a worthy and trusted companion – never a substitute for silence or direct, real, lived experience, but a support in delivering a mirror, bringing what is wordless into clearer view. And for that, I have only gratitude.

PRACTICE: Entry points

Before moving onto Part Three, pause and complete this simple practice that brings the work of Part Two into the realm of direct, personal experience. This is where these ideas become alive, grounded, and real – not as theory, but as life itself.

1. **Create space:** Find a quiet place where you will not be disturbed. Set the scene as preferred – music, candles, incense etc. Sit or lie down comfortably and close your eyes. Take a few slow breaths. Let the body settle and the mind quiet.
2. **Bring forth what is present:** Gently scan through your day, or the past few days, and let awareness reveal where there's been a charge, a discomfort, or something unresolved. Don't force or try to control what shows up – just notice it. It might be a moment of subtle irritation in a conversation, a lingering anxiety, a tightness in the chest, the mind wishing it had said this or that during an exchange, or even a slight heaviness you can't quite name. Whatever naturally arises is your entry point for this practice.

3. **Observe the mind:** Notice the thoughts that arise. Do not engage, analyse, or argue with them. Simply observe. Let the mind speak as it will, without attachment.
4. **Feel the body and emotions:** Let any emotions, sensations, or energies arise fully. Whether subtle or strong, allow them to be exactly as they are. There is nothing to fix or manage. Simply feel.
5. **Allow and release:** Stay present as emotions and sensations shift. If release begins to happen, allow it. This may come as a softening, a breath, a subtle dissolving. Let it unfold on its own. Don't try to figure anything out.
6. **Rest in stillness:** As thoughts and emotions subside, rest in what remains. No doing, no seeking. Simply being.
7. **Open to wisdom:** If it feels natural, open a dialogue with your higher knowing – whether you call it Spirit, Life, Higher Self, God, Source, or any other name. Ask, listen, allow. Let any response come freely – or not at all. There is no need to force questions or answers.
8. **Trust the unfolding:** Whatever arises is what is needed in this moment. Trust that nothing more is required and presence is enough.
9. **Close gently:** When your practice feels complete, take a few deep breaths. Open your eyes. Carry what has shifted into the rest of your day.

Summary

Part Two of this book has presented Transcending as not another practice designed to chase altered states or collect peak experiences, but as a living way to clear that which obstructs truth and return to what we already are. The four principles – observing, feeling, allowing, and releasing – provide the framework, but the real substance is in how they enable you to meet life directly as it is.

Entry points are the first appearances of a distortion that can be used as a doorway back to presence (the practice of observing, feeling, allowing). This is where the rubber truly meets the road on the way to expanding awareness. Entry points turn up the light of consciousness within. They remove the need to wait for retreats, peak states, or substances, and reduce the reliance on external teachers, gurus, or guided experiences. Instead of requiring special and often expensive conditions, they enable life itself to become the teacher – revealing what's ready to be transformed in real time, right in the middle of ordinary daily life.

A reaction in a relationship, a moment of resistance at work, a wave of emotion, even the familiar hum of subtle tension – all of these are openings for clearing. Nothing sits outside the path, because life itself is the path.

This is what makes Transcending and entry points a potent combination. It means that our practice doesn't avoid pain or postpone transformation, reserving it for special settings.

What follows isn't a high or a peak state. It's something more grounded and far more real: a stable peace, a clear sense of what's true, and a way of living aligned with the underlying intelligence of consciousness.

At the close of Part Two, it becomes clear that freedom is not something we strive towards or earn – it appears naturally when distortion falls away. Love, truth, and presence were never absent; they were simply obscured by the layers we took to be real. As those layers dissolve, the simplicity of being reveals itself, not as a concept or a temporary state, but as a lived reality available in every moment.

PART THREE

The Evolution Of Consciousness – Humanity's Future

Humanity stands at the edge of a deep inner shift. We are no longer bound to survival-based living or limited by the old illusions of mind in the way we once were. Something far more profound is emerging: a movement towards living from awareness rather than identity, presence rather than fear.

This part of the book looks beyond the practice of Transcending towards the greater unfolding it supports: the evolution of consciousness itself. Here, we'll explore what it means to live in truth – not as an ideal or aspiration, but as a lived, grounded, and embodied reality. We'll look at major shifts that arise as consciousness deepens, the undeniable kinds of experiences that may emerge as illusion dissolves, and how this inner transformation reshapes our experience within, with others, and with life.

The more we clear what is false, the more obvious what is true becomes. As this shift unfolds, both individually and collectively, we begin to see what was always so: the new era is not coming. It is already here, revealed the moment the distortions fall away.

If Part One exposed the illusion and pointed towards the truth, and Part Two offered a direct path to clearing what obstructs it at an individual level, Part Three explores what opens up naturally as that clearing becomes embodied. The journey moves beyond practice into presence, where transformation no longer comes through effort, but through alignment and resonance.

This is where the search ends – not by finding something new, but by reaching the realisation that life was never separate. It was never something to chase or fix. You begin to see that it's moving through you, as you, for you – not against you, not to you, and not separate from you. The need to control or hold on fades and what remains is a simple way of being – real, unforced, and already free.

7
A Perfect System: The Field And The Nature Of Reality

Thus far, I have made only passing reference to the field – woven through earlier chapters. We've spoken of life's intelligence, of reality mirroring our inner state, of an unseen presence behind all things. Now it is time to look directly at that presence.

What we're talking about here is the living intelligence that holds everything – what we are, beneath identity. As separation dissolves, we begin to see that life isn't happening *to* us, it's unfolding *through* and *as* us.

This chapter looks more directly at the nature of that unfolding as a lived and divinely precise system. Life expressed through the field is perfect beyond all comprehension, and its timing, its clarity, its divine precision, is beyond doubt.

What is the field?

The field is not something outside of us. It is not a mystical force to connect with or a distant energy to summon. It is the very fabric of existence – pure consciousness itself.

Every sound, every thought, every heartbeat, every galaxy turning in space – all of it arises within this single, seamless field. It is the living intelligence behind all life, the awareness in which all experience appears and disappears. The field is not separate from us or from Source – God. It is not a 'thing' that can be observed from the outside. It is reality itself – omnipresent, unbroken, without edges or divisions. What we call 'me' and 'the world' are simply movements within it, waves on the same ocean.

The field is not something to reach for. It is already here, holding everything as it is. When we sit and dissolve what is false and the illusion of a separate 'me' falls away, the field is no longer hidden. It is recognised as the only reality there has ever been – just pure, aware, and loving presence.

The essence of the field is simple, but it's so vast the mind can't hold it. It has no preference, no agenda, no bias. It doesn't resist or cling. It doesn't need anything to be different to what it is. It holds all things without being any of them. It is the sky that allows storms to come and go; is the ocean that allows waves to rise and fall.

A perfect system

The field does not make mistakes. There is no randomness in its movements. Every moment, every challenge, every meeting is a precise reflection of the inner conditions at play. What arises on the outside is always an invitation to see what is still being held inside.

This is what makes the field a perfect system. It does not miss, it does not forget, and it does not waste a moment. Even what the mind labels as 'bad' or 'unfair' is part of its precise path guiding us back to truth.

Suffering is not a sign that something has gone wrong; it is a sign that we have forgotten what we are, and that something false is ready to be seen. Hence the modern Zen saying: 'Obstacles are not in the way – they are the way.' They appear exactly where an identity is gripping on – where we are still protecting a fictional self; still surviving imagined threats; still believing in right and wrong; still caught in the feeling that something is missing, that someone or something is not enough, that peace and wholeness are found in the external world, that life should be different; and still lost in the greatest distortion of all, the illusion that we are separate and alone. The field moves for truth, and in doing so, it delivers every experience needed for this great illusion to dissolve.

The perfection of the field is not sentimental. It is not concerned with comfort or preference. Whether seen or unseen, everything is a movement of the field. Every scent, thought, body, event, encounter, sensation, emotion – all are part of a perfect orchestration that is *always* in balance, even when the mind can't recognise this or thinks something is 'wrong'. This perfection isn't about everything being pleasant, comfortable, or ideal by the mind's standards; it's about everything being perfect in its expression.

Life is perfect, just as it is. This includes you, your life, and each and every experience you've ever had and will ever have. Perfect doesn't mean right or good. It means nothing is out of place. Life never makes a mistake – nothing exists outside divine intelligence. Every distortion, no matter how horrific, is not an error but a mirror, showing humanity what remains unseen, unloved, or unhealed. The mirror asks to be seen clearly, so the pattern no longer needs to repeat. This is how the evolution of consciousness works.

Understanding triggers

When we're triggered, the reflex is often to blame whoever or whatever 'caused' our response. 'They' said something, did something, or brought something up. But the truth is simple: the self-structure cannot see itself, so it projects. It pushes the discomfort outwardly, onto the 'other', because looking inwards would mean feeling what's unresolved. If a trigger stirs fear, shame, inadequacy, or pain, the ego reacts with defence: '*You* made me feel this way.' But the person or situation didn't create the wound – they just revealed it.

Blame keeps the illusion of control and separation intact, and it also keeps us stuck. The trigger isn't a weapon – it's a mirror from the field showing us what's still buried, what's ready to be met.

Where the mind sees a threat, awareness sees a gift. Until that shift in perception happens, we remain caught in projection, missing the invitation to return inward and dissolve what's false.

This, again, is the perfection of the field at work. Not punishing, not random – exact. Every trigger is delivered with precision, not to shame us, but to free us. What hurts only does so because it touches what has yet to be healed.

Whatever we react to in another person, or in life, is a reflection of what is unseen within ourselves; the field will deliver the reflections needed with laser sharp timing. When the trigger is seen for what it is (observing), and the sensations are met with presence (feeling and allowing) the story dissolves (releasing), the charge falls away, and what is left is the stillness that was here all along.

Life then stops feeling like a series of accidents or simple bad luck and we begin to recognise its flawless unfolding. Every step, whether easy or difficult, is part of the return to what has always been real.

The mechanics of the field

The field is not separate from you – it is you, it was you before the idea of 'you' arose. What appears as 'life happening' is actually life reflecting itself. The inner and the outer are not two distinct parts – they move as one seamless whole.

This is why entry points matter so much. An entry point is simply where the field has held up a mirror for you – a thought, feeling, trigger, or challenge that reveals an unresolved pattern. What is showing up in your relationships, work, health, or environment is not random. The field presents these moments deliberately, reflecting the identity patterns that are ready to be met. The fact that you picked up and are reading this book is no random event; it's the field bringing you more of what you need to dissolve and remember the truth.

Old patterns born from fear, lack, control, or shame will keep reappearing until they are met fully and cleared. The same theme may show up in several different disguises, but will always carry the same underlying frequency. Entry points act like the hinges on the doorway to awareness – they swing open the moment you stop resisting what's in front of you. Each is a precise opening into whatever pattern has been holding the particular illusion in place. Step through it, and what once felt like a problem becomes the path back to truth. Transcending is the conscious choice to walk through those doorways, meet what's there, and dissolve it in awareness.

As soon as distortion dissolves, the reflection changes. The outer no longer needs to repeat the pattern because the inner condition that called it forth is gone. This is why a single deep release can shift an entire area of life, even a whole lineage of ancestral trauma, without forcing external change.

The field is responsive in real time. It does not wait for next week or next year. The moment you recognise the field in motion and meet a distorted moment as an entry point back to presence – feeling it, seeing it, and releasing it – the mirror is wiped clean. Life's reflection becomes clearer, not because you have rearranged the world, but because the truth within you is no longer obscured.

Examples of the field in motion

The field doesn't deal in theory – it works in real life, constantly. Its precision becomes obvious when you start seeing the link between what's happening inside and what's showing up outside and/or vice versa. The more honestly and rigorously you track that link, the more layers can be seen, met, and cleared. Let's look at some examples.

In your relationships, a particular pattern might keep surfacing – different faces, same dynamic. This will continue to present itself until that pattern is seen, and the programme and fear underlying it is finally met, felt, and released.

Maybe there's one particular conversation that leaves you defensive, or a point of tension with a partner or friend. It might feel like a subtle bitterness, resentment, guilt, or shame that only you know is occurring inside of you. This is not random; it's the field holding up a mirror.

An apparent 'failure' at work or in a project can be the outer world reflecting an inner belief of not being ready or not deserving, of needing control, or of misalignment. The setback isn't a punishment – it's the exact event needed to bring the distortion, underlying belief, and then ultimate truth into view.

And when clarity lands inside, the outer often shifts immediately. It is quite amazing when we are able to witness this divine precision in real time. A conflict dissolves because the charge that was feeding it is gone. An opportunity appears without the need to chase after it, because the pattern that was blocking it has been cleared. A new connection comes seemingly out of nowhere, and there's an immediate sense of recognition and alignment.

Your mother calls you the next day, right after you've cleared a layer connected to her. That's the field responding with exact precision – not coincidence, not magic, but consciousness reflecting itself in real time.

When you recognise the profound intelligence of the field, life no longer feels like something happening *to* you. Instead, it's better understood as a divinely perfect system, giving you exactly what you need, exactly when you need it, and it's always guiding you home, back to presence. Consciousness, life, the field – living through you and as you.

Common misunderstandings

The field is not a tool to get what your identity wants. It's not a cosmic wish list or a mental trick for manifesting desires. It is not 'the secret'. Those kinds of approaches start from the false assumption that life should bend to match the mind's preferences – but the mind's preferences are often built on fear, lack, and separation.

The field is not something you can control or manipulate. The idea of trying to control the field itself comes from a mistaken identity – the same illusion the field is designed to reveal and dissolve.

The field doesn't deal in fantasies. It deals in truth, and truth doesn't always look like the outcome we imagined – it looks like the exact conditions needed to bring us home to what we really are.

When you stop trying to bend life to your will, you begin to see how it has always been bending everything back towards reality. That's the perfection of the system – it is truly marvellous. The twists and turns, the perfect timing, the characters that come and go – none of it is accidental. We celebrate masterful storytellers like Quentin Tarantino, Ridley Scott, Martin Scorsese, Christopher Nolan, and William Shakespeare for what they create, and it can still be humbling to notice how life arranges its own scenes, with no author anyone can point to and twists nobody could have imagined. When seen clearly, it becomes obvious – divinity and the way it conducts all of life, is beyond all comprehension. Every moment, every twist of 'fate', every 'random coincidence' is part of a story far more intelligent, beautiful, and precise than a single mind could ever conjure or fully comprehend.

Living in harmony with the field

The field doesn't teach; it shows you, through reflection, what you're believing. The moment we step out of presence, life holds up the exact mirror we need to see it again.

This might show up as the ache of missing someone, or the longing for a love that never quite lands the way we hoped – pointing to the illusion that someone or something outside of us will make us whole.

It might look like fear around money – thinking there won't be enough, or we won't be OK – revealing that safety is still being sought externally rather than found within.

It can be felt as a subtle anxiety about falling behind, pointing to a hidden belief that our worth is measured by comparison of pace, progress, or accomplishment. Or a deeper fear that we're somehow not enough, exposing the hold of a core identity built around lack, shame, or needing to become something 'better'.

Sometimes it shows up as tension in a conversation, a pattern repeating in a relationship, or the pressure to prove ourselves – reflecting the identity's need for control, approval, or validation.

Or the belief that a person, relationship, success, or status, once secured, will finally make us feel safe – revealing the deeper fear we've been trying not to feel.

Whatever form it takes, it's never random. The field isn't punishing or testing – it's revealing. Every uncomfortable moment is a reflection pointing us inward, showing where the illusion is still being held onto. What feels like a problem is actually a portal. The reaction is the potential entry point, if recognised as such, and the more we learn to see what's there rather than resist it, the more life reveals its deeper order.

Living in harmony with the field doesn't mean everything goes the way the mind wants it to – it means you no longer need it to. Control gives way to trust.

Even in uncertainty, peace is present. Not because the future is secure according to the mind's ideals, but because you are resting in the same field that moves the stars, flies the bees, and beats your heart.

The tree grows, its branches reach, leaves come, and the flowers bloom – all without effort, and in their own time.

Life's got you – just as it always has.

As the illusions fall away, it becomes unmistakable: happiness isn't found in a moment, a person, an achievement, or anything external. Safety doesn't come from control, and freedom isn't something to earn. These are not conditions to chase, but qualities of what you already are. When this is lived truth, there's nothing left to push against, grasp for, or fear – life moves as it does, and you move with it. Self as Field.

Summary

The field is not something to find. It cannot be reached, gained, or summoned – because it has never been absent. It is the reality in which every experience, every breath, and every moment has always unfolded.

As the false self continues to dissolve, the field is not revealed as something new, but recognised as what has been here all along: the seamless intelligence holding everything. Nothing has ever been outside it – not happiness, love, safety, or the moments we considered mistakes or detours.

This is the thread running through the whole journey of this book: the shift from searching for life's truth outside of ourselves to living *from* it. The field has been the background of every step, every challenge, and every breakthrough. It is not just the context for our lives – it *is* life, moving as all of it. When that lands, the sense of something missing starts to dissolve.

8
Life Beyond The Illusion

When enough clearing has taken place, you can begin to live from a different place – not from the restlessness of the mind or the strategies of the identity, but from a grounded way of being that no longer latches onto effort, image, or outcome. This shift isn't always obvious. More often, it is profoundly simple – a return to what has always been present, free from the distortions that once obscured it.

Many expect the search to bring them inner peace, mental clarity, better relationships, or a deeper sense of purpose and while this is often true, it is not the essence of the change. The real transformation is in what falls away: the exhausting ambitions and never-ending striving, the old beliefs, the fixing, managing, and endless becoming, one fear after another, and the playing of fictitious roles that once felt central to our life. What seemed personal is seen as irrelevant. What once needed proving no longer matters.

This chapter points to what reveals itself when the core illusions have lost their grip, and when truth itself – this moment, this breath, presence, life as it is – is finally enough.

The core illusions that unwind

No longer chasing some future state of being or an improved self, life begins to unfold from a deeper place. The mind quietens, identity loses its charge, and a silent intelligence starts moving everything like the river flowing back to the ocean.

The deeper the clearing moves, the more obvious it becomes that life has not been about becoming something better, something new, or 'something' at all, but about remembering what is and has always been real beyond the endless illusions. Central to that remembering is the unwinding of the subtle identities that once held everything in place – often naturally, unnoticed, and without fanfare.

While many illusions collapse along the path, there are a few that tend to sit at the core of the human experience. These are not just beliefs – they are entire mental structures and self-images, woven deep into the nervous system, playing out in every relationship, every ambition, and every emotional trigger. As these begin to dissolve, something radically simple takes their place: truth, reality, unburdened by story. What follows is the unravelling of some of the most central illusions as identity fades and consciousness rises. Let's take a look at some of these common illusions in turn.

The illusion of love

Of all the illusions that dissolve on the path to awakening, love may be the most deeply ingrained and difficult to unravel, because it feels so deeply real. It is embedded in every memory of connection, every wound of the past, every desire to be held, and the longing to be seen, understood, or chosen. What most people call love is not only something they chase but something they build their entire identity around, believing that to be loved is to finally be whole, complete, and happy.

Put plainly, most of what we call love is not love at all. It's a survival strategy – trying to feel safe through another person.

From our earliest years, we are conditioned to associate love with approval, attention, affection, and safety. Without realising it, we come to believe that love is something external – something that must be earned, and that can be taken away. Thus it becomes a transaction to manage, a feeling to protect, and a fragile condition we hope to secure. If the right person comes along, if the perfect connection is forged, if we are finally loved the way we imagine we can be – we will be safe. This idea becomes the ultimate goal shaping our relationships, behaviours, and even spiritual beliefs.

It fuels the impulse to perform, to chase validation, to abandon ourselves on the promise of being chosen. It plays out in fantasies, in fears of rejection, in the exhausting pursuit of 'the one' who will finally meet the unmet need inside us.

The illusion of love continues within the spiritual realm, repackaged as divine union, twin flames, the soul, cosmic or intergalactic agreements – but the root distortion stays the same: the belief that wholeness is found through meeting with another.

That longing for a union, for intimacy, is rarely about the other person – it is the field's memory of wholeness calling itself home. Beneath the surface-level images and fantasies, it is not 'you' seeking 'them', but life remembering itself beyond that early separation. The draw toward closeness is the call of the truth that there is no gap to close, no distance to cross, no division to heal. It's the same force that pulls a wave back into the ocean, confused as the desire to merge with another.

When this pull towards union arises, it can be used as a doorway back to presence. Instead of following the mind's images and stories about who or what will make it feel fulfilled, pause and feel the raw energy of the longing in the body. Notice its texture, its movement, and where it gathers. Let it be there without trying to fix it, act on it, or turn it into a plan. In this way, the longing no longer drives an impulse to go out and find something or someone to complete the self; instead, it becomes a living reminder to return to what is already within you. By staying present with the sensation, breathing into it, and allowing it to unfold without resistance, the pull to 'find' resolves into the recognition that nothing is missing and that this, right now, is enough. Perfect as it is. The apparent emptiness the longing points to is actually the spacious awareness in which everything appears. This is intimacy in its purest form – being fully present with and accepting of what is, without needing anything to arrive or change.

The confusion and complexity around the illusion of love is built on one simple but significant misunderstanding: love is not a feeling to grasp or a bond to preserve. It is not something given, lost, or proven. It does not exist in certain people, in certain moments, or in certain forms. It is not emotional, not personal, and not based on need, exchange, or agreement. When this 'mind-love' is tied to being wanted, accepted, or understood, it shrinks into something less, something conditional. When it is seen as something that can disappear or be taken away it is no longer love – it is longing and fear dressed up as love.

The truth of love

As the illusion dissolves what's left is, again, what was always here: the silent presence that remains even when relationships can't meet us in truth, and/or when they fall away. The energy of longing begins to slow, the need to be chosen loses its grip, and identities built around being loved or unloved begin to fall apart. In the stillness that follows, something pure and real can emerge – not as a belief, but as reality.

In truth, to love is not to *feel* a certain way. It is to allow all things to be as they are, without resistance, control, or judgement. It does not involve fixing, changing, earning, or deserving. It is the living and loving field of presence that holds it all – the longing and the loss, the joy and the grief, the clarity and the confusion. When this is known, not as a concept but as a lived reality, the search for love and completeness in the external world comes to a natural end. Relationships are no longer vehicles to complete the self but expressions of what is already whole. There is no fear of being alone, because love no longer depends on proximity or agreement. Even when a person leaves, the love does not go – it was never theirs to give or take. It was never about them. It was always right here.

When we say 'I love you', it seems as if the love belongs to the other person or is somehow coming from them. In reality, their presence is the stimulus, not the source. They are a mirror that brings the depth of your own being into awareness. The warmth, tenderness, and openness you feel around them are movements of the love that you are. This is why the same quality of love can appear with a partner, a friend, a child, a stranger, a tree in the forest, or a cat on your lap. The forms differ, but the field is the same. Seeing this clearly loosens the grip of attachment. You can cherish the person without confusing them for the source of the love that is shining. The source can't be owned – it's simply what remains when the need to secure love falls away.

It is not wrong, though, to want to share love with another. The beauty of human connection, of intimacy and devotion, is real, but it cannot be found 'out there' unless it's first discovered 'in here'. Any attempt to reach for it externally without first coming home to it within, will reinforce the illusion of separation. That doesn't mean relationships are unimportant – it means that they are most blissful and joyful when they arise from a way of being that is already full, not from the need to be completed.

This is why love makes no distinctions between worthy and unworthy, mine and yours, past and future. It asks for nothing in return, not even to be seen or recognised. It includes and makes space for everything, even the illusion and emotional pain of not being loved, and holds it all without needing it to change.

The ultimate truth of love, then, is simple. Love is the nature of reality itself. God and love are not separate.

God is all. Nothing exists outside of God, and nothing exists outside of love. Even the idea of separation, even forgetting, even fear, and even pain – it's all held within it. Love, therefore, isn't something that comes and goes. It is never missing and it is never elsewhere. It's what you are.

Awareness is God's love – pure, unconditionally inclusive, and unbound by time or circumstance. It is the silent, ever-present reality in which all experience appears and disappears. When the mind's search falls away, there is only *this* loving and aware presence – self-shining, self-complete, and inseparable from the love that is God.

Look now, take a breath. Love doesn't need to be found – it's already here.

If the longing for love arises, let that point you inwards: don't chase it outwards. Sit. Breathe. Observe. Feel. Allow. As you meet life as it is and let it be the way that it is, you are coming back to the love that is already here. That's all you need to do. The field will take care of the rest.

The illusion of money

The illusion around money is not about income, numbers, or the practical need for resources to live. It is the identity built around money, the sense that who we are is tied to being secure, successful, independent, abundant, generous, worthy, enough or 'on track'. Even in groups that reject materialism, money becomes charged with meaning. It is used as a sign of alignment, worthiness, spiritual maturity, trust, or 'flow'.

When money appears, the mind feels safe. When it tightens or disappears, the mind assumes something is wrong. In this way, money becomes a mirror for the identity – a proxy for survival, belonging, dignity, and the imagined right to exist.

At the core, the illusion around money is simple: the ego believes that money keeps it alive. It fears that without controlling money it will lose freedom, identity, respect, options, worth, even life. This fear is ancient and primal, but it is not true. Life is not supported by a currency we created; it is supported by the same intelligence that moves breath through the body, lifts and drops the tides, and spins the planets. When this is seen, the emotional grip many people have around money – whether they have lots of it or not – loosens. Money returns to being a tool, not a source of identity or safety. It can be flowing or not, present or absent, predictable or not, without disturbing one's inner state.

To put it simply, real freedom cannot be bought; it is what is present when the illusion that anything is required to secure your being falls away.

The truth of money

The truth about money is uncomplicated: it is neutral. Money is not a sign of security, worthiness, alignment, or spiritual maturity. It cannot measure your value or confirm anything about who or what you are. Some of the wealthiest people are the most burdened, and some of the poorest live in profound peace.

Many assume that once they 'have enough', they will finally feel safe. But safety does not come from a number. Money is not the source of security – life is. Money comes and goes like weather. It is part of the movement of life, not the meaning of life. When the illusion dissolves, money is used with clarity. It flows in when it flows in, flows out when it flows out, and none of it creates or removes your inherent freedom. The mind no longer panics or celebrates based on what the numbers say. Safety is no longer outsourced to the bank balance or an employer. Identity is not built upon it. Life is no longer spent doing things out of fear of not having enough.

As money is seen clearly – as a tool rather than a truth – life becomes lighter. Yet this clarity stays out of reach for many, because it demands a level of surrender the mind cannot fake. Freedom appears when it is wanted more than the illusion that protects us from it.

This isn't about giving up money; it's about letting go of what you believe money makes you. It's about giving up the illusion that money gives you your being. You don't surrender money – you surrender the identity built around it. When that dissolves, nothing is lost except the fear that kept you trapped.

The illusion of purpose and contribution

Alongside money, the illusion of purpose is one of the most persistent identities the false self holds onto. It begins innocently: the desire to help, to matter, to do something meaningful. But underneath, the same mechanism is running: the drive to become someone. The mind is constantly looking for ways to keep itself busy.

The identity fears being nothing – irrelevant, unseen, unneeded. It panics in silence or stillness. It grips to direction and mission, because without them, it feels like it might explode or disappear. Even after awakening begins, this illusion can survive. It simply reshapes itself into spiritual language. Purpose becomes 'dharma'. Impact becomes 'service'. Identity becomes 'embodiment'. The core fear endures untouched. This is why many sincere people end up working relentlessly in the name of contribution, while still feeling restless, unseen, or not enough. The ego has simply taken on holy colours.

At its heart, the illusion of purpose says: *I must become someone meaningful to be worthy.*

But you cannot become what you already are.

The truth about purpose and contribution

When the illusion dissolves, purpose stops being something to seek. It is no longer a role to fulfil, a mission to find, or a storyline to protect. It is not earned through helping, working hard, sacrificing, serving, or leaving a legacy. None of that makes you valuable.

Your value is inherent, and nothing needs to justify your existence. Being is already enough. When movement appears, let it arise from presence, not the mind. One creates another illusion to pursue; the other is the natural expression of what you are. Purpose then becomes something completely different – not something you do, but something that moves when nothing is in the way. It is the natural flow of life through an unburdened system. There is no performance; no rush; no pressure to matter; no need to be seen, followed, admired, renowned, or even remembered. Who cares? Only the identity, and it is fictitious.

Instead, you move when movement is true; you stop when stopping is true and contribution happens, or it doesn't. Neither adds to or takes away from who you are. In this way, meaning is no longer figured out, chased, forced, or manufactured. It is recognised in the simplicity of being.

Purpose is not a pursuit of the mind; it is what remains when the pursuit ends. This is where all doing happens for its own sake, without trying to prove, to matter, or to become anything. It moves because it's true, nothing more.

The illusion of identity

Identity is the core illusion. The one that can outlast every insight, every breakthrough, every transformation, and every collapse of belief. It doesn't just hide in what is seen; it hides in the one who claims to be seeing it. It isn't loud and it isn't obvious because it feels like you. That is how it slips past even the sincerest seekers, even the teachers, even the 'awakened' ones.

It's not just another illusion to clear; it's the one that holds the whole system in place. Every story about love, purpose, healing, devotion, or awakening orbits around a central, unquestioned assumption: that you are a someone. A separate, individual self who is doing, becoming, controlling, living life, and ultimately, trying to get somewhere.

At first glance, identity looks like your name, your history, your personality, your preferences, your roles. But these are just surface ripples. Beneath them are more subtle identities; those carefully constructed but ultimately fictional self-images that have been driving your decisions, reactions, and relational dynamics for as long as you can remember. The high achiever who needs to win. The fixer who needs to help. The spiritual leader who needs to be seen as free. The humble friend who needs to be seen as not needing anything from anyone. The people pleaser who needs to be liked. The seeker who performs presence. The imposter who fears being found out. These patterns form identities that provide the mental structure of who you believe yourself to be.

Some of these identities are common and well-recognised, such as the victim or the villain. Others are more refined and can be socially rewarded:

- The good listener
- The wise guide
- The loving friend
- The smart counsel
- The success story
- The saviour/hero
- The independent thinker
- The humble teacher
- The awakened soul
- The survivor
- The giver
- The clear communicator

- The one who sees what others can't
- The one who is 'beyond ego' – but is still clinging to a subtler form

These self-images are not bad or wrong. They are protective structures; survival strategies shaped by early conditioning, emotional pain, culture, and our need for coherence and safety. The traits that make up these self-images are not randomly determined. Somewhere along the way, the mind decides: *This is how I stay loved. This is how I get seen. This is how I stay safe.* As we live and evolve, a new, more refined identity appears, then another. It's like cutting off the head of a snake, only for a new head to appear, or sometimes more than one...

In this way, the mind holds on. Even when you know you're not your story, not your role, not your trauma, there is a self-image that holds in the background, adjusting, improving, spiritualising, and performing an identity.

Even on the path to awakening, the image gets a new tattoo, adds some feathers, and upgrades its wardrobe. The seeker becomes the finder. The victim becomes the healer. The helper becomes the embodiment coach. The one with all the questions becomes the one with all the answers. The spiritual identity can take the form of wisdom, stillness, presence, or even silence – believing themselves to have transcended, while still needing the 'fact' of this transcendence to be known by others.

It can even appear in the writing of this book and in the way these words want to be received.

This is all happening in the background. It's not personal – this is what the ego does, and what it does well. Ego doesn't care what the identity is, as long as there is one.

You may notice it in conversation. A quiet urge to appear clear, or free, or unfazed. A need to sound informed, to ask a profound question, or to offer just the right reflection. Maybe you catch yourself in a little white lie, embellishing a story to make it more impressive or the subtle urge to say 'I know that already'. This is the self-image managing how you show up.

You may notice it in withdrawal. The one who used to need to be liked now needs to not need anything. The one who used to chase approval now distances themselves from anyone who might trigger their old identity. The effort to have no image can itself be an image. Even the quietest, most humble, peaceful version of self can be a mask held up to keep it safe.

If you're now wondering whether and how this is still playing out in yourself, notice what feels threatened. Notice what you defend, what you avoid, and what you subtly position. It's not always loud. Often it hides in the quieter moves: calling something 'intuition' when it's actually avoidance; labelling distance as 'boundaries' when it's protection; performing humility to avoid exposure. If something needs to be maintained, protected, justified or explained, or visible – this is a sign that a self-image is at play.

You'll feel it in the body before you catch it in the mind. A flicker of contraction in the chest. A tightening in the gut. A sudden tension in the jaw behind the words you're about to say. The face tightening as you listen, holding a polite smile while someone's words trigger something deeper. A slight lean forward when pushing, explaining, proving, or making your point, or a physical withdrawal into silence. These are subtle signals, revealing not that something is wrong, but that there is still a need to survive, belong, or be seen a certain way. Watch for those moments and use them as entry points – they'll show you everything you are ready to see.

This illusion of identity is not a flaw, nor anything to judge – it's the final defence mechanism of the overarching illusion of separation. The self-image persists until it is fully seen for what it is: a mental overlay, not an essential truth. A structure of belief and habit, not a real self.

But this illusion is heavy. Holding it up is exhausting. It's like carrying a fragile sculpture on your back – every movement shaped by the fear that it might crack or fall. Relationships, work, even spiritual practice become subtly distorted as you protect and polish it. Carrying its weight, you begin to notice how many decisions are made not from clarity, but from the image you are trying to maintain. How many conversations are guided not by presence, but by the need to protect, to be liked, to be right, to be wise, to be healed, to be good, or even to appear beyond it all.

Eventually, if there is enough willingness and courage, the identity is seen and collapses slowly, bit by bit, under its own weight. In the space where it once stood, only the simplicity of presence remains.

The truth of identity

When the illusion breaks, it becomes obvious how futile it is to keep rearranging your self-image or polishing your 'character' in the hope that one day you'll finally approve of who you see in the mirror. No identity will ever be whole enough, strong enough, or complete enough – because what you are is not an identity at all.

Awakening doesn't erase the personality or necessarily turn you into a silent monk sitting on a hill. The human expression continues, with its humour, its timing, its quirks, its way of speaking or moving. The difference is that it's no longer mistaken for who you are. The character still plays its part, but without the weight of identity, lack, defence, performance, or illusion. Life expresses through you freely, instead of you trying to shape yourself into something. Nothing essential is lost; what falls away is the belief that the personality is you.

You are not a separate one waking up. Waking is here. You are not a separate one seeing. Seeing is here. You are not a separate one having experience. Experience arises and dissolves in what is here. You are not a separate one evolving. Becoming unfolds without a controller.

Not the fixer. Not the teacher. Not the spiritual one. Not the broken one. Not the one who gets it. Not the one who doesn't.

Clouds pass. The sky is what it is.

Again, this is not something to believe or adopt. It is a direct recognition – so clear, so intimate, that the entire illusion collapses the moment it is truly seen. The seeker, the struggler, the teacher, the guru, the role, the voice, the need to perform, to help, to be seen, to prove anything, to *be* anything – it's all a projection of the mind that dissolves into what has always been here: awareness, presence.

This is what Jesus meant when he said, 'Before Abraham was, I am.'[19] He wasn't referring to a person or claiming a spiritual title. He was pointing directly to the timeless truth of being itself. To the reality that what you are was never born and cannot die.

The self you believe yourself to be – the one with a past and a future, a story and a wound, a calling and a contribution – is a mirage, a fiction. What's real is what's here before the story: simple awareness, the capacity to know experience as it arises. It was here before thought, before identity formed, and it doesn't come and go.

'Before Abraham was, I am.'

When this is seen, what is left is not a perfected self, but the *end of self* and the end of the search. Not a better version of you, but freedom from needing to be anything at all. The mountain you were climbing disappears and with that, so does the climber – it was all an illusion of the mind. You move from being a someone, to a no one, to only *one*. Not as a concept or identity, but as the direct recognition of what you are: pure being.

There is no longer anyone to protect or project. Conversations flow without a manager. Action arises without a strategy. Love moves without fear. Life unfolds as itself, without needing a someone to control it. This is freedom – not *for* the person, but *from* the person.

The illusion is that you are a *someone*: a fixed identity, a character with a history, holding a place in time, moving towards some final form. The truth is what's here before that story: awareness itself, not as a new identity to adopt, but as the simple fact of knowing.

It doesn't belong to 'you', because the 'you' that claims ownership is part of the story. It isn't separate from you either, because what you actually are was never a separate someone in the first place. It only looked hidden behind the belief in being broken, imperfect, or apart from life – instead of seeing that life is already living itself.

The illusion of control

The ego's deepest comfort comes from believing it is in charge – deciding, choosing, steering life towards the outcomes it wants and away from those it fears. We call this free will, but most of our 'choices' are not free at all. They are conditioned responses – patterns set in motion by genetics, upbringing, memory, emotion, habit, and the momentum of countless prior causes.

Again, this illusion persists even in spiritual practice – in the belief that if 'I' adopt the right techniques, think the right thoughts, or make the right moves, then life will unfold in my favour. This belief is false. It's much like an avocado tree believing it can choose to grow bananas if it tries hard enough.

Every decision becomes a test, every result a verdict on personal competence. Success inflates the sense of self; failure threatens it. But in truth, both are the mind claiming authorship over what is already unfolding on its own.

Like a leaf believing it is steering the river that carries it away, the separate self imagines it is the doer when in reality, it is one with the current. The thought 'I am deciding' arises after the movement to act has already begun. The feeling of control is just another appearance in awareness, not proof that there is anyone behind the wheel.

The truth of control

Life lives itself; it never needed a manager or controller in the middle. Once this is seen, the burden, stress, worry, and exhausting weight of the illusion of control drops. Life moves as it always has – on its own, spontaneously, perfectly, and without effort. Action occurs without the tension of believing 'I' am making it happen. This is not fatalism or passivity – it is a deeper participation in life's unfolding that occurs once the false centre has dissolved. Real freedom is not found in 'controlling' the flow, but in realising there is no one apart from it who could control it. You are not even the one flowing; flow simply arises.

In brief, the illusion of control is dependent on the false belief that you are a separate self moving through life. What's true is simpler: life is already moving, and the 'me' that claims authorship is part of the story

The illusion of more

As awareness deepens, the striving that is driven by the ego naturally comes to an end – not because the goals were reached, but because the one who was striving is gone. The search for more, whether in worldly or spiritual terms, is recognised as just another movement of the illusion.

We've been conditioned to chase – more success, more status, more security. Again, the spiritual path can present another version of this: more insight, more awakening, more stillness, more ceremony, more medicine, more of anything that can prove and validate how conscious we are. But at some point on the path, the one chasing, proving, and seeking burns out and disappears, and the illusion of there being 'more' to attain dissolves.

The truth of more

True presence doesn't require achievement, ceremony, performance, or any kind of becoming. It's the natural end of all striving. This is total surrender, and it is as profoundly simple as it is liberating.

A short story captures the essence of this truth. It's a modern parable based on a 1963 story by Nobel laureate Heinrich Böll, that has been retold countless times in various ways.[20]

A businessman on holiday in a quiet coastal village noticed a fisherman resting beside his small boat in the morning sun. Curious, he asked why he wasn't out catching more fish. The fisherman explained that he had already caught enough for the day. The businessman suggested that if the fisherman worked longer hours, he could buy a larger boat, hire a crew, build a fleet, expand globally, and eventually make millions. The fisherman paused and asked, 'And after that?'

The businessman said, 'Then you could finally relax and enjoy your life.'

The fisherman smiled. He was already doing exactly that.

The story points directly to the illusion that there is 'more' to be had – that the happiness we seek is somewhere ahead, waiting at the end of achievement. It is only ever here. It has always been here.

We chase 'more' out of fear that life as it is could never be enough. But the real more is not a quantity – it's a quality. It is the depth, richness, and fullness that becomes available when the mind stops seeking. Presence does not limit your life; it unveils the dimension the mind has no access to – the one where nothing is missing.

The illusion is that fulfilment and happiness live somewhere in the future, after the right relationship arrives; after enough money is secured; after enough impact is made; after we've done, achieved, or proven enough. The truth is that nothing is missing now. What you are is already here – complete, silent, and free from becoming.

When it matters most

A few years after beginning this work, it became real to me in a very different way when my father passed. He had been diagnosed with terminal cancer. On my birthday, he called and I answered expecting a 'Happy birthday, Son' but instead he simply said, 'This is it. Can you come home?' and hung up. Three days later I got back to the UK and arrived at his hospice bedside; he was no longer responsive, but I knew he could hear me.

We had healed our relationship some ten years earlier, and I was deeply grateful that we had remained close ever since. I thanked him for waiting for me to get back to him, for giving me life, and for the way he'd carried himself through his final months. There was nothing left unsaid. We then sat together in silence, with me touching his arm and face, simply being together. The falling away of old stories I had projected onto him had long since cleared away the pain of our past. There was an understanding and connectedness between us. In the end, all that was there was love and compassion, without obstruction.

As I sat in meditation with him, holding his hands, I told him, 'Know that you are loved, know that you are forgiven, and know that you are not alone. Thank you for waiting for me, you can go when you are ready.' His breathing deepened, then softened, and gradually slowed until eventually it stopped. He died peacefully with his hands in mine, having held on until I'd got back. My brother entered the room just after and we hugged and cried, in both grief and relief.

This was one of the most profound experiences of my life. Not because of any special technique, practice, or state, but because there was no resistance left. Everything had already been cleared between us. There was no fear, no resentment, no regret, and nothing left unsaid. Only love, acceptance, compassion, and gratitude.

This, to me, is an example of the real reward of this work. Not spirituality as an act, or consciousness as a concept or badge, but the freedom to meet life's most sacred moments with nothing in the way. The work of Transcending is not about chasing states or polishing a spiritual self-image. It is about expanding awareness and removing what distorts truth so that, when life calls for it – at a bedside, in grief, in despair, in confusion, or in love – you can meet it fully, being present, open, and without bitterness, resistance, attachment, or fear.

Death and completion

The deeper we go into the reality of life, the clearer it becomes: death is not a threat to what we are. What dies is only the body. Life itself abides – love, awareness, God expressed through form, never separate, only appearing to be so. In that knowledge, even death becomes just another wave passing over the surface. What we truly are can never die.

And yet, while there's no need to fear death, there is still something to honour before it comes. Not out of pressure or punishment, but out of the integrity of truth. Life will always move to balance itself. Whatever has been avoided, denied, or held onto will rise again – not to torment us, but to be released. It's not about fixing the past or reaching some final state; it's about using the time we have to meet what arises and let it clear, so we don't carry unnecessary suffering to the end.

To meet death with peace is to meet life now – fully, honestly, lovingly – so that when the body drops away, there's nothing left unspoken, unfelt, or unresolved. There can then be just a natural return to what we've always been.

Summary

As consciousness expands, the illusions that once defined reality begin to dissolve. Not just intellectually, but at the level of direct experience. It becomes clear that what we once pursued – love, purpose, wealth, safety, control, identity – was never needed, never missing. The suffering was never of life itself, but was created in the mind's attempt to find peace through becoming someone.

Each illusion carries a promise: that if we just get it right, find the one, fulfil our calling, achieve enough, survive enough, prove enough, improve enough, do enough, or become the best version of ourselves, we'll finally 'arrive'. But the only thing these pursuits ever reinforce is the belief in a separate self who needs to get somewhere and be someone other than what it already is. Whole, perfect, complete.

The end of illusion isn't the end of becoming – it's the beginning of *being*. Of being fully here, simply as you truly and already are.

9
Openings Beyond The Mind

In the course of deep spiritual practice, there are times when the body and energy system shift in ways that can feel miraculous, even otherworldly. These spiritual experiences are often spoken of in mystical language, with wonder and awe. Across traditions, such events have been revered, pursued, and sometimes treated as the pinnacle of the spiritual path itself.

These kinds of rare experience can be utterly holy and wholly indescribable. But even so, they are not the goal. They are natural byproducts of removing what obscures the essence of what we are. As identification with the mind and the conditioned self dissolves, the body's energy, perception, and entire system can reorganise in ways that reflect this deeper alignment. For some, these shifts are subtle, for others, they are unmistakable

– waves of energy surging through the body, bursts of inner light, visions, or the piercing of an unseen veil.

The purpose of this chapter is to bring clarity to something that is rarely discussed; to share lived experience, to demystify these events by explaining, to the best of my knowledge and intuition, what they are and what they are not, and to point to the truth they can reveal. Every genuine opening carries the temptation to form an identity around it, to make it a possession, a badge, or a spiritual achievement. The ego-mind will take any opportunity it can to create a specialness that will counter a sense of lack.

Experiences such as Kundalini awakening, inner visions, or the opening of the third eye will be explored more fully later in the chapter. For now, what matters is understanding their role: they are not achievements to chase but invitations to deepen surrender.

These events remind us that life itself is moving, realigning, and clearing distortion to allow presence to know itself more fully. These experiences are not an endpoint. They are not personal, but part of the same unfolding that can be met in any moment – in the rhythm of an ordinary breath, in the quiet of a simple day – without the need for fireworks, fanfare, pedestals, glorification, or creation of content.

What follows is only one set of lived experiences. It isn't a template, a promise, or a measure of where anyone 'should' be. By the end of this chapter, the focus returns to the only real question: how is this grounded and lived, right here, in the ordinary, including in the places that press the deepest buttons, like family?

Understanding the energetics

While the search for enlightenment and the rising of Kundalini are linked, they are not the same. The energy is often described as a dormant spiritual energy coiled at the base of the spine, waiting to be awakened. While traditions use different metaphors, in direct experience it is less a 'thing' to be activated and more the natural flow of life's energy when the obstructions begin to dissolve. As the mind's grip loosens, false identities dissolve and old emotional contractions are released in their own time, this energy can rise through the central channel of the body, enlivening, and reorganising the whole system.

In yogic traditions, the 'third eye' is symbolically linked to the sixth chakra, *ajna,* and associated with the pineal gland – a small endocrine gland deep within the brain that regulates circadian rhythms through melatonin production. While science does not and cannot confirm mystical claims about the pineal gland, in spiritual practice the third eye is not understood as a physical organ or a magical switch, but as an energetic centre.

When this centre 'activates', there is a shift in perception itself – awareness expands beyond the surface of appearances into subtler layers of reality. There can be a direct window into patterns, energies, and the essence beneath what is seen by the two physical eyes. This may arise as symbolic or archetypal imagery, as inner light, or as a clarity of sight that feels less perceived and more known.

Neither Kundalini rising nor the opening of the third eye are external gifts or rewards. They are the body and consciousness coming into alignment, and the nervous system recalibrating to reflect the absence of identity. As the conditioned self dissolves, the system naturally reorganises itself in ways that may be experienced as surges of energy, bursts of light, intense shaking, full body takeovers, energetic transmissions, and visionary openings.

While such shifts are indescribable in experience, they are simply what happens when the inner architecture adjusts to reflect truth. There have been many of these experiences over the years – far more than I can track. Some of the early ones have already been shared. The ones that follow arose later in the journey, and include the surge of experiences towards the end of the search. They are described in the order in which they occurred.

The first signs

Long before there was any formal name for the practice that I would later refer to as Transcending – perhaps two years before I even knew what it was – a different kind of movement began to show itself.

In moments of deep meditation or during the release of strong emotion, my body would shake. At times, it was subtle, a gentle tremor moving through my frame; at others, it was so strong that my whole body seemed to be taken over for hours on end, as if something deep inside was trying to break free. The most noticeable activity was around the heart centre. There were surges, pulses, and waves of movement in that space, often accompanied by a sense of release or relief, though without any conscious intention to make it happen (although this typically occurred during meditation).

For a time, it felt like stress leaving my body; like a lifetime and even ancestral tension finally finding a way out. But as the months went on, something shifted. The movement no longer felt like a release of the old. It began to feel like the arrival of something new – an intelligent energy moving through like a system upgrade, repairing, restoring, rebooting, and reorganising my configuration from the inside.

These episodes came and went with increasing frequency over a period of four to five years, not tied to any specific technique or goal other than meditating, then through Transcending, and ultimately through a genuine surrender to truth. Certain words could bring it on, like 'God' or 'love', not by just saying the words, but by feeling their essence.

An early opening

It was around two years into deep, sustained clearing through the practice of Transcending and meeting life directly through entry points – and a few months into studying the later trilogy by David Hawkins[21] – that the deeper architecture of illusion began to reveal itself more clearly. Patterns that once felt personal I now see to be universal. Long after the initial intensity of spiritual searching had fallen away, an experience arrived the way true openings often do: completely unexpected and unannounced.

While lying in practice, my body suddenly became a conduit for an immense rush of energy. It surged upward into my brain, concentrating in the region of the third eye. The force of it was intense – strong enough to completely take over my body's movement and attention – yet there was no fear, only trust. A deep knowing that this was life itself moving, and that nothing could be out of place.

There was no thinking at all. Not the quieting of thought through effort, but the complete absence of it – as if the machinery of identification had been switched off, albeit temporarily. It felt as though thought itself was being dissolved, or that the link between awareness and the mind's stream had been cleanly severed. I can best describe the sensation as like floating in the clouds.

In that space, there was no 'me'. No character to maintain, no story to uphold, no past or future. Just pure being, pure awareness – weightless and exquisitely at peace. There was no sense of the passage of time, only the direct experience of stillness. It was an unspeakable and wordless state.

When the surge of energy eventually faded, something fundamental remained changed. The quietness of the mind did not leave. Even while functional thoughts returned, they no longer carried the same pull of identification. Early in the mornings and late at night – times when there was nothing to be done – my mind would fall entirely silent again.

This shift came only after a long period of inner clearing and dissolution, yet it happened in an instant, without warning. At this point I had only vaguely heard of the third eye. It was not something I was looking for or seeking to 'open'. And yet, it began to activate – on its own, unasked for, as a natural movement of life when nothing was in its way. These activations would increase in frequency and intensity over the years that followed.

A perfect storm before the calm – a transformative relationship

Just over a year after that first activation, with countless activations since, I had let everything go. All public work, all outward sharing, property, car, belongings – everything that was no longer aligned with what I now knew to be truth. All expressions of 'being someone' in the world were falling away. Life had moved me into a different rhythm – one that required stillness, not structure.

A major part of that letting go was a relationship unlike any I had known before. From the beginning, there was a sense that this meeting would be different. It was the container for total transformation. A space where both of us, deeply committed to the path, were willing and able to face everything that arose.

Surprisingly, one of the most important decisions I eventually made was to remain celibate throughout most of that relationship. This choice came from a deeper wisdom and clarity. So much was unravelling on the inside and, eventually, the space between us no longer felt clean enough for me to continue with intimacy in the normal sense. I had reached a point where I couldn't enter that kind of connection without a clear, conscious foundation. The choice to remain celibate wasn't easy, but it felt right. It created even more space for the deeper work to unfold; this brought its own kind of intensity, but also a level of honesty and stillness that allowed the process to deepen in a very real way.

This was a relentless three-year unfolding – a crucible of growth, heartache, and love, bumping up against every pattern, a commitment to clarity, and a fight for truth. It held both the deepest most beautiful connection and the sharpest most painful edges. It brought to the surface layers that couldn't have been accessed alone. Transcending became a lifeline in the midst of that overwhelming, exhausting intensity – an experience that, as one might imagine, offered no shortage of entry points.

There was so much love between us. It was the meeting of two pure hearts doing their best to break free of suffering. There were all the familiar hopes and attachments – that perhaps this could be the one that lasted. However, somewhere deep in my body, there was always a sense that it couldn't be. Not just that it wouldn't, but that it *couldn't*. What we had to put each other through, what we had to face together, what had to rise in the space between us, most people could not, and would not, walk through. Simple as that.

At its core, I was looking to her for peace, and she was looking to me for safety – and the relationship became the space that had to deliver these things. But peace and safety can't be sourced from another person, so the bond turned into pressure, scanning, and disappointment, instead of simple love.

This wasn't the relationship that could endure, but it was the one that would complete something. The final entanglement in a long karmic chain of unconscious, painful, necessary, and beautiful relationships.

Relationships have always been a central part of the path for me. I've never been attached to staying in one that didn't feel fully aligned. Many have come and gone over the years, each playing a major role in the search – as a mirror, a teacher, a gift – and each bringing forward the next level of integration. This particular connection was no exception, but it also carried something unique. Its depth, intensity, and the courage it demanded shaped my path in a way nothing else had before. As powerful as it was, when it finally reached completion, we were both able to recognise this and, eventually, let it go in complete trust, love, gratitude, and acceptance. Of course there was intense grief, sadness, and heartache but I eventually understood what that pain was about – the burning away of the illusion that happiness would come from anything or anyone outside myself – so I could meet it fully. I knew the karmic contract between the wounded masculine and wounded feminine had finally been fulfilled.

That connection will always be honoured – for the part it played, and the truth it helped reveal. But that part of the clearing was complete.

From the pain of that ending, a profound shift began. I entered a period where I was no longer available for a relationship, choosing instead to meet and resolve what had always been avoided, and to see what could never be seen while I was still engaged in relationship. I had nowhere else to go but within. The completion of that relationship became the catalyst for an even deeper seeing that could only unfold in solitude. I was being prepared for something entirely new to emerge, the most sacred of all unions: not with a person, but with life itself, met directly, without separation.

Disappearing into Self

At this point, I found myself living temporarily off-grid in a conscious community deep in the Costa Rican jungle. There was a profound sense of gratitude that life had placed me there. I didn't need much – somewhere clean to sleep, something clean to eat (fresh coconuts were a welcome daily delight), and the occasional moment of connection. Most of my time was spent in stillness, alone, in nature. That land, that silence, that chapter was the perfect calm ground for what was to come next.

My presence there wasn't random. It was orchestrated by the same intelligence that had always guided the journey, placing me exactly where I needed to be, at exactly the right time, with exactly the conditions required for the next layer of illusion to dissolve. Life is perfect and the field always delivers.

In this calm, I could feel the momentum of the world falling away. There was no desire to return to any role, identity, or any form of structured life. I longed only for simplicity and imagined disappearing into a quiet life – completely at peace with fading from the world.

I could sense a deeper pull to completion still moving through me – like when an animal instinctively knows it's about to die and finds a final corner to rest in. I felt like that.

Rakta Bindu transmission – opening of inner seeing

Soon after arriving in the jungle, I took part in a sacred ceremony, a drop of menstrual blood – known in some traditions as *Rakta Bindu*, or 'the red drop' – was placed directly onto my third eye. In that instant, a massive surge of energy shot through my entire being, bypassing the mind completely. I let out a primal scream – loud, raw, and uncontrollable. Not from pain, but from an unexplainable force erupting through my body. It looked like a reaction, but it was a release.

This was not a usual response, and, at the time, there was no logical explanation for what moved through me because what moved through me wasn't of the mind. It wasn't about whose blood it was, or a ceremony to understand at a conceptual level; rather, it was a doorway to direct knowing through readiness. It wasn't 'me' screaming – it was life itself, remembering itself through this body.

I staggered off into a corner and sat with my eyes closed. In my mind's eye, it looked as though I was speeding, faster than light, through the entire universe. More screams came and primal tears tore through everything that once held the illusion of separation in place.

The scream was the sound the body makes when it finally connects with the full and unimaginably brutal sensational ache of separation. I felt it – like the entirety of human suffering screamed through me. The sweetness and joy that immediately followed was the dissolution of that separation. It was the body's raw response to the unbearable pain of having once believed it was apart from life, now collapsing into the truth that this was never so. In that moment, the reality of 'not-two' was not an abstract idea or even 'known' – I felt it in my cells and in my blood. It felt like the collective grief of humanity meeting the relief of finally coming home.

This was pure yin meeting pure yang; the essence of creation (feminine, menstrual blood, womb, source of all form) meeting the essence of perception (masculine, awareness, the unchanging witness). Yin, the deep fertile dark, and yang, the bright illuminating light, touching in one place – the third eye. When these two energies meet, and when conditions are ripe, something unimaginable moves. While incredibly rare, when it occurs the body can only scream, weep, or collapse – because the meeting is total.

This was not the kind of awakening people romanticise, or that you often hear about. This was primal, core, visceral, ancient, utterly unexpected, and undeniable. It was pure transmission from the field.

Full-spectrum awakening

A week after the Rakta Bindu ceremony, the field moved again – this time in a way that was more sustained and more all-consuming than anything that had come before.

It began in stillness late at night lying in my cabin in the jungle. What unfolded that night moved because the system was finally permeable enough to receive it. I had taken a small amount of LSD that night. What unfolded went far beyond anything I could reduce to chemistry. Without warning, energy overtook the third eye area and my body entered a state unlike anything I'd ever experienced. My eyes completely rolled back and my entire system began to vibrate. Energy surged upward in a continuous wave, flooding the third eye with a power beyond words. My body was no longer under my control – the full and unmistakable presence of life itself had taken over.

I felt as if I were physically dying, literally vanishing back into source, and in that instance of recognition, I snapped myself back into the room. The sheer fear and confusion of what was dissolving was so overwhelming that, for the second time since the awakening process had begun sixteen years earlier, a part of me pulled back. It's entirely possible that this was the complete dissolution of the self, but facing the possibility of death, I simply wasn't willing to take the chance – I did not feel ready for death at this point. This was the truth of where my system was in that moment. But even without crossing that last threshold, the shift was irreversible.

As I resettled into this state – my eyes rolled back again and my body resumed its shaking – visions began to move through me: not imagined, not dreamed, but alive, vivid, and charged with meaning. I saw intricate geometries of light, moving with an intelligence that felt older than time. It was the architecture of reality itself – patterns of pure consciousness taking form. Out of this arose a frequency of absolute unity, and the knowing came: *'I and the Father are one.'* These words weren't thought – they were beingness speaking itself into me.

Then, the images shifted. I was no longer watching – I was inside the vision. I was Jesus on the cross, not as a character in a story, but as the living embodiment of surrender, forgiveness, and the total yielding to life's will. There were flashes of Bethlehem – not as a place on a map, but as the symbol of the divine being born into form.

Other visions followed. I was in a vast hall, surrounded by enlightened beings welcoming me home. Their presence was overwhelming, yet familiar. Then, it was as though their energy flooded my body. This wasn't imagination – it was transmission. The wisdom of the awakened field poured directly into me.

The energy then dropped into the root, vibrating with pure life force. It felt like a reseeding – the primal creative energy of the universe awakening in the body. It was foundational, as though life and truth itself were rooting fully into form. Then came the sacred union. Not like romantic or sexual union, but the sacred union of life with itself – the balancing of yin and yang, the integration of the masculine and feminine within, the unification with Source. This was the restoration of wholeness – not as an idea, but as direct experience.

Finally, I saw myself giving through the eyes alone – no doing, no effort, no role. Just the gaze transmitting presence. It was the clearest recognition I'd yet reached that true giving doesn't come from will, but from the pureness of being.

Much more occurred, more than can be explained because, as is the nature of such transmissions, words completely fail to capture the experience. What moved through me was not meant to be captured. Around four hours passed on the clock, though within the experience time ceased to have meaning. There was no 'me' deciding or managing. The mind had no foothold, 'I' was not in control. There was only movement, unfolding as it needed to. Eventually the visions receded. I returned to the room and my body gradually stopped reverberating until finally it was still and I could move again. But something fundamental had shifted. Two weeks later, I sat in an Ayahuasca ceremony. Its message was simple: no more medicine, no more substances.

The archetypes of awakening had played out through my mind and body – not to tell me who I was, but to show me what I am. At first, my mind could only take these literally. Was I seeing past lives? Was I remembering something historical? It was utterly overwhelming to say the least. This is where many get lost – mistaking the symbol for the self – and I too was in shock, completely struck and lost for words. But as the hours, days, and weeks passed, the meaning of the visions became clear: these were not memories, but archetypal transmissions. The crucifixion I'd seen was the death of identification. The visions of Bethlehem signalled the birth of the divine union within. The message was not 'you were that' but 'this is in you now'.

This full-spectrum awakening was the convergence of multiple profound shifts in awareness all at once – the full rising of Kundalini, the activation of the third eye, the embodiment of Christ consciousness, the opening into archetypal visions, and the sacred union with and *as* life itself. It was not any kind of final, permanent, or arrival event. Rather, it was an experience of the illusion of separation dissolving across mind, body, heart, and spirit, revealing the seamless presence of life. Over time, this understanding continued to deepen and integrate, with each unfolding bringing new clarity and embodiment. Even now, writing this, it sinks deeper and becomes clearer still.

In its simplest expression, the unknowable and the indescribable took over.

Third eye opening

In the weeks that followed, I entered a long, unplanned period of silence and solitude. It wasn't a vow or a practice, just the quiet that naturally comes when more and more is seen and released. There was no urge to speak. The mind had lost its grip, and what remained was pure spaciousness.

One day, I felt that Kundalini was rising again and, with it, came a vision of my skull cracking wide open. From the opening, a flood of light poured out and up, as if my head could no longer contain it – it was quite terrifying. The next day, in the silence of night, lying in bed, I felt the familiar surge of energy rising into the third eye but this time it felt different – more complete, more total. It wasn't building toward something. It *was* something.

Again, my body and head were completely taken over. Then came the very physical sensation of something like a laser moving down my forehead, inch by inch – hot, precise, intense. It burned, but not in a way that called for resistance. It was the burn of being fully opened. I was in the presence of the energy of life in its purest form – unseen yet undeniably real. The burn slowly carved down and pulled open the space above and between the brows, as if making a permanent opening. This was not imagination; it was a felt, sensed experience. There was no thought and no insight or interpretation. Just pure presence, suspended in vastness, like floating in space without a body.

This was not another third eye activation. It was a full opening.

The 'third eye' isn't some mystical symbol we imagine – it's a genuinely felt, sensed, experiential shift in perception. When the third eye is fully open, the mind stops relying on the five senses alone and starts knowing directly. It's not about gaining special powers or chasing visions; it's about removing the filters that twist reality.

Awareness allows us to see without the fog of interpretation.

The heat or carving sensation I described is not literal, but it was felt – it's how a nervous system being rewired feels to the body. The 'light' is the natural radiance of awareness when nothing is clouding it. When this opening stabilises, the old sense of 'I'm here and life is out there' begins to fade. Seeing becomes pure – life seeing itself, through itself.

From that night onwards, presence was no longer a passing experience, but it took time to fully settle into it. There was a period of integration – learning to live with this new way of perceiving – until it became the natural, unbroken way of experiencing life. This deep integration is ongoing.

Three months in the jungle

Three months in the jungle opened the space for all of this to unfold. A three-week stretch of complete silence, during that time, opened into a depth of stillness that revealed what had been waiting beneath a lifetime of noise. Many of the experiences I've shared happened in that silence, when nothing was left to distract the system from what needed to move.

Other openings came through the reflection of human contact – conversations, presence with others, and the shared field revealing patterns and truth in real time. It wasn't the jungle itself, nor the people, nor any substances or ceremony that created these movements. It was the readiness. The jungle simply offered the perfect conditions: solitude, slowness, humility, and an uninterrupted intimacy with the field. I'm deeply grateful for that time. And after three months, it was clear the movement was complete. There was nothing left to seek. It was simply time to go.

Integration and living truth

These experiences, while extraordinary, were never the point. As someone who had never chased any of them in the first place, this was obvious. They just happened, as natural occurrences and doorways to living beyond illusion. And while I can attempt to describe them, what they were ultimately doing is impossible to fully know – the mechanics aren't mine to explain.

Real integration comes in the quiet after the storm. The wild, uncontainable surges gave way to something far more ordinary, yet infinitely more valuable: living deeper in presence, particularly in the ordinary moments of life. Not the kind of presence that arrives with fireworks, but the kind that is simply here, and whenever identity tries to reassert itself, presence isn't lost – it's available the moment it's noticed.

In that presence, the doorways remain the same as they were before the first flicker of energy: observing, feeling, and allowing. But now this happens automatically and more naturally. Whether the body is still or shaking, sitting or lying down; whether the mind is quiet or active; whether light is flooding the skull or nothing remarkable is happening at all, presence remains.

Coming full circle

After these seemingly miraculous experiences came something else: there was a much quieter sense of a peace. Stillness. Bliss. It felt like the culmination of everything.

I had followed the pull into the deepest shadows, devoted myself to truth, and now I felt the absence of striving, seeking, or story. There was no desire to return to the world.

I returned to a now familiar urge – to live in a monastery, ashram, or spiritual community and disappear permanently. I observed how the mind imagined these paths as some kind of natural or obvious next step. But it was just more mind, and when even those ideas were dropped, what revealed itself wasn't a cave or a temple. Something completely unexpected opened up: home. Not home as a concept or a memory, but the literal place: Scotland, my mum's house.

I had left Scotland twenty-five years earlier. Since then I'd seen the world, lived in many different places, and lived many different lives. I had dissolved countless layers but something in me knew that the next part of the journey involved coming home – not just metaphorically, or to a physical place, but to a person. I wanted to connect with my mum from the clear space that I was in now. I wanted to be not just a son dropping in once or twice a year, but to be fully present with her in real daily life. When you only see someone rarely, what kind of relationship do you really have? In such circumstances, that which is deeply buried beneath the surface never gets a chance to rise. This felt particularly relevant to me given how long I had been living away.

There was an obvious sense that, for reasons both known and unknown, it was time to go home at least for a while. The field was moving again and the timing felt precise, so off I went.

Observing

What unfolded when I got there surprised me. I found myself face to face with the earliest layers of identity – the source pattern I didn't even realise was still in my system. The energy in that home, and especially in my relationship with my mum, brought up something in my nervous system that felt very old. Patterns I didn't know existed or thought were long gone were suddenly reactivated in the space between us.

It was as chaotic as it was subtle – like a reflex I hadn't fully outgrown. Something mostly dormant, but when the right point was touched, the reaction was immediate – fast and automatic, like something still wired in.

Being back home after all that had transpired was humbling and grounding. There was a depth of awareness that was almost surreal. Contrary to the presence cultivated within, it felt like I had stepped back in time. The environment and circumstances had obviously changed but certain energies and patterns had not. Some conditions were almost identical to those I'd grown up in. But now I wasn't a child trying to survive, escape, or rescue anyone. I was present and intensely aware of what was happening beneath the surface.

I could see it all so much more clearly. The programmes, the conditioning, the familiar patterns that had shaped how we related to one another and the old relational dynamics still playing out. My childhood made more sense than ever before, including the experiences of those around me. Mum, Dad, my brothers… it was as though I could feel it from their side too. Like I had touched the core of it – not just my story, but the whole system that story had grown out of.

For the first time, I could see my mum with a clarity and compassion I hadn't been able to access before. My mum has a heart of gold, and I could see that her way of surviving had been to avoid feeling, to push it down and keep moving. Fear and hurt were carried because that was the only way she knew how to function. With nowhere safe for those feelings to go, it seemed that parts of her had gradually closed over time as a way of protecting herself. The system looked for release wherever it could – sometimes through tension, resistance or misunderstanding. Dad had the same approach and, of course, the same survival pattern, in different forms, had shaped the wider family dynamic. At the same time, I could feel a sense of what my dad must have been going through within himself and within the dynamic – not to excuse what he did, but to see more clearly the human being beneath the violence, a man without the tools or capacity to meet life any better than the only way he knew.

While the harm he caused was real, the fuller picture was far more complex. Realising this was both eye-opening and quite heartbreaking. I realised that through my efforts to protect my mum, I had wrapped her in a ball of cotton wool for most of my life, which had made it almost impossible to see the whole picture clearly. I could never have understood what she went through, how affected she still was, or how hard she was finding it, because I simply hadn't spent enough real time with her to see it. Being back in close contact made these things obvious. I realised I'd been relating more to a hopeful fantasy of who I wanted or needed her to be, and that was humbling to see.

I could also recognise how deeply my mum and dad had fit together: how their wounds locked into one another, and how their survival strategies continually triggered each other. They had been a perfect match, at a vibrational level, for the life they were destined to live. After all this time, I was finally seeing clearly, and in that kind of seeing, something vast revealed itself – how intricately and intelligently life weaves everything together. How perfect it all is, even in its pain. How it always takes two. And how sobering it is to rediscover that the stories we see, or hear of, are rarely the whole truth.

It was beautiful, painful, revelatory, triggering, challenging, and ultimately, perfect.

Feeling

The overall process of observing this reality was not easy and it brought up a lot of familiar emotional triggers and mechanisms. My mind struggled initially. It did try to make certain situations about her but, again and again, I brought it back to the truth: this wasn't about her – it's never about anyone else. It was about something still unresolved inside me. That's when I began to truly see just how embedded this pattern had become.

I began to notice how deeply I'd internalised the role of 'the one who wants peace'. The one who makes it all OK. The one responsible for my mum's happiness. It wasn't conscious, and at the same time, it was completely ingrained. My system, through its own reasoning, had been trained to fix, protect, and absorb. I could see that every time I stayed in situations that felt overwhelming, I wasn't honouring her, I was dishonouring myself.

There is so much love and care between me and my mum, and I had always been so grateful for her. She had always been loving, always been there for me, and we had each others' backs. She was my biggest cheerleader and the one and only person who had been a consistent loving presence in my life since birth. But I could see now how much of my identity had been shaped around trying to keep her safe and happy. Being back home, I could see it wasn't working anymore – for either of us. My system would automatically move into saving and fixing, and her system would automatically tighten into defence. Nothing could really land, and it created a clash that was revealing and necessary for both of us.

My system was on fire and I could feel it burning. There were feelings of anger, resentment, frustration, and, underneath that, sadness – and to my surprise, guilt.

Allowing

I stayed with these feelings; I didn't run. I let the discomfort rise again and again, over and over. I sat in the fire of all the old roles that being around her was bringing to the surface and I observed and felt the guilt as it surfaced again and again. The guilt that said, 'If she's not OK, I've failed. If she's suffering, I should fix it. If I can't fix it, it's my fault; I'm not a good son.' I had already seen where and how that story had been born, but I hadn't realised how deeply it had embedded into my system until now. I observed and felt it fully.

Of course, it had never been my job to hold her life together, and she'd never asked for that. It was just old code – the primary imprint that had influenced my entire life, projected onto past partners, even expressed through my work – and I was here to see it all fully and finally, to let it burn out once and for all. It was never real, it was never needed, and it was never mine to carry. She was the way she was, whole and complete – nothing wrong and nothing to fix. My work was no longer to turn her into someone else, but to relate to her as she was and to be honest about what I could and could not stand.

Looking more closely, I could see the core equation that had been written into my nervous system as a child: if Mum was OK, I was safe; if she wasn't, my very existence felt under threat. My peace, happiness, and safety were unconsciously outsourced to her state. That early wiring became the template for everything that followed – partners, places, spiritual highs, and work. I wasn't just trying to help her; I was still living from the belief that what I was seeking lived outside of myself.

Being home in this immersive way was the most advanced and challenging spiritual work I had ever engaged in – it seemed I had been preparing for this my entire life. There were moments when I wanted to cut off, to protect myself by stepping away completely. That had been my strategy in past relationships but I wouldn't do that here. Of course I took space when it was needed, but I knew I had to face something and I felt the readiness to do so.

So, I trusted the life that had brought me back and I stayed firm, and let life do its work. I stayed in the fire and purged, letting it burn intensely until it extinguished itself. I let go over and over – not of my mum, but of the role in relation to her that I had identified with. I allowed my nervous system to feel safe without needing to fix or change anything. I began to see her journey as hers, between her and God, just as mine was between me and God. I dropped the expectation that our time together should feel a certain way. I let it all be what it was.

Releasing

Finally, I could let go of the fantasy that things should be easier. I felt and released the idea that I could go home and be untouched. I grieved the version of her I thought she needed to be and then, underneath all my pain and suffering, I found something deeper. I found the presence that doesn't need anyone to change. The love that knows how to say 'no' and doesn't depend on harmony. The peace, acceptance, and compassion that is present, even when things are tough.

A new reality dissolved the only one my system ever knew: 'This was never mine to carry. I am safe. So is she. There was nothing to fix, nothing to control. Presence is enough.' I learned to let my mum be exactly as she is, and how to put in clean boundaries without blame, guilt, or drama.

What then became unmistakably clear was that my peace had never been in her hands. It had only felt that way when I was a child. Her challenges, her pain, her fears, were the stimuli that showed me what I was ready to see. They lit up the old child filter inside me that said, *If she's not happy, I'm not safe. I won't survive. I need to do something*. That was the whole knot right there. Seeing this allowed me to feel the panic, attachment, and fear, directly, where it was truly born, to let it burn, let it go, let my mum be exactly as she was.

It wasn't blissful or transcendent. It was a slow grind and, in many ways, the most brutal part of the journey so far – raw, messy, human, and necessary. It made everything else feel like a dress rehearsal. Over a very intense year, with plenty of breaks in between, inside that immersive spiritual dojo called 'home', the first and most ingrained imprint – *Happiness, peace, and safety lives outside myself* – was finally and fully dissolved. The more I let go – of guilt, of roles, of responsibility, fear, and attachment – and the deeper I used my mum's stimuli as a mirror to see myself, the more I purged, the more it cleared, and the more I settled into presence. The more I settled there, the more my mum also settled in her own way – in my presence, she could finally see more of herself, too, and she was open. Without pressure or force, the illusion that my peace depended on her began to loosen its grip, and a natural ease returned between us. Day by day there was more spaciousness, lightness, laughter, and patience too. That didn't mean the house became the perfect expression of harmony or that our dynamic suddenly felt easy all the time. Some moments were still challenging. But a different baseline was emerging in me, and the bond between my inner state and hers was slowly and surely disappearing. At the time of writing, what once triggered reactivity has largely settled into neutrality.

Clarity eventually showed me that the real struggle was never with my mum. It was with the illusion of separation itself – the subtle mental split that turns life into 'me in here' and 'you out there'. Once that split is assumed, relationship becomes a project. There is something to fix, heal, resolve, or complete. The identity comes online automatically because a separate 'me' now seems responsible for the outcome. In this structure, comparison appears, then evaluation, then effort. Emotional charge follows as a natural consequence. Guilt, responsibility, resentment, and fear are symptoms of the illusion of divide (subject–object) doing what it always does.

As this was seen clearly, something fundamental shifted. There was no longer a 'me' in relation to my mum that needed to manage her state or secure my own. Without that assumed position, the charge had nothing to attach to. Interaction continued, moments still happened, feelings still arose, and old patterns still surfaced at times, but they no longer organised the field or defined the relationship. There was clarity instead of management, and a natural ease that didn't come from effort or trying to be kind, but from having no position left to defend at all.

This final imprint was clearing. Nothing needed fixing anymore.

Presence

While it is true that nothing takes you out of presence faster than the people who wired your nervous system in the first place – especially when they are still very much living their patterns – it is also true that nothing else can bring you deeper into presence than when you are finally ready to meet it fully, without needing to defend, explain, or fix. It's grounding, real, and even hilarious at times. Finding the comedy in it all, where possible, was natural medicine for us both.

In this 'final' return, something had settled. What had once felt like an impossible knot had now been lived, seen, released, and accepted for what it was. Nothing was left undone and so nothing more was needed.

Through it all, what also became clear was just how strong my mum is. Her path was not easy, and she carried more emotional weight than anyone would knowingly want to carry, yet she endured. She didn't collapse under it or let it consume her; she simply kept going, doing the best she could with what she had. Through everything, she was a devoted mother and her kids were everything. Seeing her more fully, without the distortions of childhood, only filled me with love and compassion.

I could also let go of the idea that her journey should mirror mine or that any path was better or worse. Her path was never about awakening the way mine has been. It was about surviving, enduring, loving no matter what, and birthing a new generation – one that now births a new generation of its own. That, too, is sacred. She had the strength to carry out what life asked of her, and she did that fully.

Seeing it all so clearly wasn't like waving a magic wand – it meant recognising, in real time, the exact moment the 'me' reappeared and started turning the relationship into a problem to solve. When that was seen clearly, the compulsion to manage dropped on its own, and each time it unwound a little more. What remained was just what was here: sensation, emotion, presence, and the freedom to let my mum be as she is without needing to manage, fix, or control anything anymore.

When all was said and done, I was there, she was there, love was present, the space was ever-clearing, and that was enough. What once stirred fear, guilt, reactivity, anger, or frustration had become something else entirely: an opportunity to deepen into presence, to meet each moment with patience, have a real relationship and make the most of the time we had together even if it was messy from time to time – that's human, nothing more than that.

It is the primary caregiver that makes the first imprint on a child, and so it makes sense for this to be one of the last ones to dissolve. Coming home wasn't a retreat from the world. It was precious time with my mother, and it carried a depth I can't really explain. It completed something in me that only being there in that way could have completed.

Reality

Whatever our stories, whatever our struggles – with other people, ourselves, directly with family or indirectly passed along the ancestral line – this is life. Not a mistake or a detour, but life as it is being lived through us.

Some have fought to be seen, while others have learned to disappear. Some have carried the weight for everyone else, while others have grown accustomed to staying small, strong, or silent. Many of us have also learned, without ever choosing it, that our peace and safety depends on someone else's state – a parent's mood, a partner's approval, a teacher's affection – and spent a lifetime chasing externally what was never actually outside of us at all.

No two childhoods are the same, because life isn't trying to produce one outcome. It isn't organised for a single template of healing or awakening. It's organised for all possibilities. Some of us get warmth; some get distance. Some get stability; some get chaos. One isn't 'better' than the other. They're different arrangements of the same intelligence, shaping different lessons, different strengths, different ways that love learns to come home to itself.

In family ties, this is especially revealing. Nothing needs to be forced. The past doesn't need to be rewritten. When the sense of a separate 'me' isn't running the interaction, the charge loses its fuel. Then there is simple seeing, appropriate response, and tenderness. No longer identity to identity relating, but essence to essence instead.

However it played out, the path was never random. The pain, the roles, the patterns – all of it served us, all of it shaped us, and all of it brought each of us right to this point.

The mind may wish it had been different, or grieve what could have been – but the truth is that nothing was ever out of place. What it called 'broken' was never so. It was all part of the mysterious unfolding – perfect, precise, sacred, and divine.

We come into this life having forgotten what we are, and through every experience – every wound, every pattern, every relationship – life invites remembrance. If we say yes to that invitation, healing happens, growing happens, waking up happens, and returning happens. This is divinity, remembering itself through form.

Every meeting, every wound, every pattern was perfectly placed in the grand tapestry of life, woven with a precision far beyond what the mind can grasp. Seen from that view, what remains is simplicity, acceptance, a well of gratitude, and deep compassion, for ourselves, for our families, and for the beautiful, tender mess of the human experience – what a trip!

And at the heart of it all, there is only love – not the love we chase, protect against, or fear losing, but the love that's always been here at the core of our being. Boundless and unconditional. Closer than breath. Not separate from God, because it *is* God. Reality unfiltered. Beyond all interferences of the mind. The greatest illusion is that you could ever be apart from it, and when this is seen, the idea of being separate falls away on its own.

Summary

Transformative spiritual experiences, however they are labelled – Kundalini rising, Christ consciousness, third eye opening, transmission, sacred union – can sound, look, and feel extraordinary. They *are* extraordinary. But their essence is natural, not supernatural. They don't arise because we chase them; they arise because we stop chasing. When the blocks clear and the noise of self fades, life moves in ways the mind could never imagine, plan, or produce.

The real integration of awakening is not something to seek or protect, but something to live. It shows in how we meet the ordinary. It shows in the kitchen, the car, the living room; with the people you didn't choose but were given, and the ones you chose and can't escape.

In whether we defend or dissolve, resist or rest. And, still, the most important place of all: within. Freedom isn't measured by what we've seen or realised, but by how we show up when the dust settles.

No matter the pattern – whether it's the seeker, the fixer, the knower, the one who hides, the good son/sister/father/mother, or the one who waits – when it all finally falls away, something simpler returns. A way of being that is quiet, present, and fully human *being*. Nothing left to prove, protect, or perfect. No longer managing, fixing, needing anything or anyone to change.

That's where peace and freedom stop being ideas and become a lived, felt, and known reality – in the here and now – prior to mind.

10
Calling In The New Era

Something unprecedented is happening. Humanity today stands on the edge of a transformation that is reshaping not just how we live, but who we know ourselves to be. By remembrance and returning to what has always been true.

This new era is not a future ideal – it's here, unfolding now. We see it in those who have stopped playing roles, those who are living from presence, and those whose lives are stepping out of conditioning and shifting from fear to love. The message may still sound faint to the wider world, but its presence is undeniable – the frequency has changed.

The new era doesn't mean a world full of perfected beings or a planet where everyone has dissolved the ego. The new era is quieter, more human than that. For many, it will simply look like less numbing and pretending, more honesty, responsibility, and care. For others, it will unfold as a clearer recognition of their spiritual nature and a life lived with more peace, connection, and love. And for a smaller number, there is a different kind of pull: to follow this all the way through to the end of seeking and the dissolution of the separate self. This chapter speaks to the end of the search.

What follows is not a grand theory but a simple map of this transition. First, we will look at what this new era points to – the movement from mind-led living to life moved by aware presence. Then we will shine a light on one of the last defences of the old consciousness: the subtle spiritual ego that hides inside awakening itself. Finally, we will explore how this shift actually lives – through Transcending, through alignment with the field, through the end of seeking and the ordinariness that remains for those called to walk that far.

This chapter is less about ideas of the future and more about how this new humanity is already being lived, in many different ways, here and now.

The next stage of human evolution

In 2009, something broke open inside me. A moment of inner awakening that changed the direction of my life. Every seeker has their first taste of awakening, though the first is seldom the last. It's rarely a 'one and done' experience, and how it stabilises varies. Either way, it is a doorway – a flash of thunder and light beyond the mind. It's the beginning of something real – the first step into a new kind of seeing.

While the unfolding never ceases, one thing can and will for those who are most committed: the suffering. When the core of illusion dissolves, suffering is no longer necessary. There will be more openings, more layers, more refinement, but the moment the identity falls away, the search can finally stop. Until then, the call to all seekers is clear: keep going.

For centuries, *Homo sapiens* – the rational, thinking human – has been seen as the pinnacle of evolution. But this is not the endpoint. It is one stage in a much longer arc. Depending on how far back you look, human evolution spans from 300,000 to over 7 million years, gradually moving through countless stages and forms.

What comes next is not only an expansion of intellect, but an expansion of aware presence. David Hawkins spoke of this transition during various lectures and in his writings, calling it the rise of 'Homo spiritus' – consciousness freed from the limitations of the personal self.[22] The term deeply resonates and points directly to the emergence of a new expression of humanity, one that recognises its spiritual nature, no longer bound by the illusion of separation, identity, or unconscious survival.

Whatever label we give it, it is clear that we are moving towards becoming a new kind of human being. A life aligned with truth and a being no longer moved by mind but guided by the deeper intelligence of love and life itself.

This is not a claim that everyone will live from this space in the same way or to the same depth. It is simply the direction in which consciousness is maturing – some will touch it in moments, some will live from it more consistently and a few will be drawn to let it guide their entire life.

The awakening of a new humanity

Humanity is beginning to shift, not through changes in biology or advances in technology, but through a recognition arising in individuals. It isn't the birth of something new, but a shift in consciousness. The old framework of thought, identity, belief, and striving is falling away slowly, and moving in is something deeper – an intelligence that doesn't need to be named, only lived. At this point, life is no longer filtered through fear, control, or separation. It's met as it is, from what we are.

This change is happening in real time. Although still rare, people are waking up – not through effort or belief, but through direct recognition. For some, the mind is beginning to loosen its grip, and the old self is dissolving, opening to something more grounded, more honest, more whole.

New generations are arriving already more sensitive to truth. Some are less interested in playing out illusions, or chasing status like their parents may have been, and they're not driven by survival like their ancestors. They're wired for clarity and kindness and can't pretend not to see. They don't need to search for what they are. They know it, even if they can't yet explain it in words.

But this isn't about age. Whether someone is twenty or seventy, they feel the same pull. When something real is heard, there's an instinctive recognition – like remembering something long forgotten. It was always here, waiting. You're ready when you're ready, and life will respond the moment you are.

Transcending as a bridge

If we strip away any framework, teaching, or label, what's left is simple. This whole path is nothing more (or less) than clearing that which blocks the natural movement of life and the truth of what we are – it is a return to presence.

Awareness is not something to develop or create – it's already here. We simply need to make the space for it to be seen, felt, and lived. To this end, Transcending is not a technique to learn – it is a bridge to this way of being. By simply recognising reflections from the field (via entry points) and sitting deeply in presence (Transcending), we can dissolve the patterns that bind us to the old self and live from what is already here.

This is a total embracing of our deeper nature. Shadows that once felt threatening become doorways to truth. Challenges are no longer detours from awakening – they are the path itself. Life is experienced as a perfect expression of divinity that is trusted to live itself through us.

As this new era unfolds, one of the most important tasks is to see clearly how the old consciousness tries to come along for the ride. The false self does not disappear just because it has learned spiritual language or adopted spiritual forms; it often relocates into the very spaces that point to freedom. What follows is not a critique of spirituality or seekers, but a clear look at how identity survives in its most refined forms, and why seeing this honestly is essential if this new era is to emerge cleanly within you.

The subtle 'spiritual' ego

For the most devoted seeker of truth, many 'final' hurdles will appear. We've already touched on the masks the ego wears, how it reshapes itself to survive even the most sincere spiritual quests. But now, as the illusion of a seeker begins to dissolve and truth comes even closer, something more precise can be seen.

At this stage, it has become clear that the illusory self isn't always loud; it can also be quiet, composed, and incredibly convincing. Once the obvious forms of attachment, control, or validation have been seen through, the identity doesn't disappear – it adapts and it evolves. It learns the language of awakening. It adopts the posture of presence. It wears the look of humility. It speaks about love and the truths it has heard, memorised, and intellectualised – sometimes beautifully – while still unknowingly protecting a self-image.

Sometimes, it hides in uncertainty – a quieter, more self-conscious expression of self. It can appear as someone trying hard to be worthy of love. They second-guess their clarity, lean on other voices, and constantly seek reassurance that they're on the right path. It might look like endlessly quoting other teachers, listing all the books and retreats one has attended, or gently inserting spiritual-sounding phrases to appear safe, aligned, or 'in the work'.

This version of the subtle identity doesn't dominate the room – it tiptoes through it, hoping to be seen as enough. Rather than posturing as enlightened, it often performs humility and spiritual sensitivity. It can appear as almost too happy, or be excessively grateful, endlessly apologetic, or overly inclusive – not because it's fake, but because the self-image still needs to be protected. This form of ego is not inflated, but defended. Not loud, but seeking. A contraction around a self still trying to be clear enough, spiritual enough, awake enough, good enough.

Then there's the other side of the spiritual ego. Not the unsure, approval-seeking self trying to be worthy of awakening, but the more confident self that's convinced it's ahead. This version often hides behind a polished and refined spiritual character – 'the one who knows'. It might not lead thousands or sit on a stage, but in everyday conversations it subtly takes the higher ground. It interrupts and explains without being asked, wanting to be seen as insightful. It gently corrects others, interprets their experience, and offers truth from above rather than beside. It drops names – the guru it follows, the shaman it sat with, the lineages it is part of. It points to retreats, fasts, diets, ceremonies, trainings, and initiations as proof of depth. None of these things are wrong in themselves, of course, but when they become badges of identity, they are all making the same claim: 'This is who I am. Please see me.' Underneath, the same fear is running the show. The self-structure is not afraid of being unsafe – it is afraid of not existing at all. Everyone is simply trying to find their way back home.

The refined identity expresses itself in infinite ways along the path. The invitation here is simply to see it for what it is – a self-image trying to secure itself – and not mistake it as proof of arrival. Don't build an identity around it. The form is not the freedom. The moment it's used to prop up an identity, especially a spiritual one, the illusion keeps its grip.

Sometimes it hides in substances and medicine, always needing the next journey, the next purge, the next opening. It seeks intensity over integration. Ceremony and plants can be supportive until they become the new addiction and/or escape – another way to feel enough, safe, special, and for the mind to keep itself busy searching.

The spiritual ego appears in 'conscious' communities as gossip, projection, blame, cliques, and the performance of presence – often the same patterns as everywhere else, simply dressed in spiritual language and spiritual costumes. It critiques teachers and teachings with a subtle superiority, calling it discernment. It surrounds itself with others on the path, but never lets the illusion of self fully die. It wants to be someone who's 'getting awakening right', and it's trying hard to achieve this.

At its highest level, the spiritual persona wears the robe of the teacher. It no longer seeks approval from peers or validation from ceremony; it feeds instead on reverence. It speaks softly, pauses intentionally, carries itself as one who has 'arrived'. It publishes great works, has mastered the art of presence as performance and it has the 'followers' and 'success' to prove it. Words are measured, gaze is unwavering, posture is serene – but underneath it all lies a quiet dependency on being seen as special.

We also play a part in this dynamic. The refined spiritual identity cannot survive without an audience willing to place it on a pedestal. When we see someone as more special, more enlightened, or closer to God than we could ever be, we are not seeing them clearly; we are often projecting our own power onto them. It can feel safer to believe that somebody else has 'arrived', and that simply being around them will somehow get us there too, so we don't have to face the uncomfortable truth that the same awareness is already here in us – and the inconvenient truth that the real work cannot be outsourced. Putting teachers and gurus above ourselves is often a way of avoiding responsibility for our own seeing and practice. The pedestal is a mirror: their willingness to sit there and our willingness to sit here. It reflects both their remaining identity and our own belief that we are somehow less.

In its more extreme expressions, this dynamic can become deeply harmful. History is full of spiritual communities that began with genuine insight and ended in distortion – financial exploitation, psychological manipulation, sexual misconduct, even abuse of those who trusted the teacher most. The details differ, but the pattern is familiar. A person has a real opening. People feel it and gather. Over time, the identity of 'the one who knows' fuses with power, money, sex, and unexamined trauma. Without honest mirrors, boundaries, or accountability, the structure becomes an echo chamber that protects the identity instead of the truth. What began as a doorway into freedom slowly turns into another prison, for the teacher and the students alike.

This is not about demonising teachers or movements. It is a cautionary note about seeing how convincing the spiritual ego can be, and how easily genuine openings can be co-opted by identity when they are not met with radical truth, courage, and humility. The same movement lives in all of us in subtler ways. Seeing it 'out there' is an invitation to look more closely 'in here'.

Furthermore, this highly refined spiritual ego claims to know the way, yet needs followers to confirm its place. It rejects hierarchy, yet subtly reinforces it through tone and distance. It says 'we are all one', but still moves as a separate 'me'. It uses humility as a disguise, silence as control, and love as leverage. When challenged, this master of disguise is exposed as it defends its fragile sense of self behind the language of consciousness – 'you're projecting', 'you're not ready', 'you don't understand yet' – or it exerts such a 'power-over' dynamic that people simply do not feel safe enough to question it.

It may teach what it knows to be true, while privately protecting its position as the one who knows. It hides in praise, in the glow of devotion, in the illusion that to help others is to be free from need. It gathers circles not only for the joy of sharing truth, but also for the energetic confirmation that it is the source of that truth. It feels safe only when the mirror is showing it to be wise.

If you get close enough to the subtle spiritual self, the cracks begin to show. The aura of serenity wavers. You feel it not in their words, but in the current that runs underneath: a subtle superiority, a lack of warmth, the absence of true patience, the appearance of arrogance, or the subtlety of 'look at me'. There's often a hidden edge, a faint sense of manipulation or control disguised as guidance. They may speak of love but move with an agenda; speak of surrender but subtly demand devotion.

The deeper truth is simple: when real presence is met, it feels safe, kind, and non-hierarchical. When it's not, you can feel the contraction – the air thickens, the heart closes, and something in you knows: this person is still trying to be someone. The real thing doesn't have to prove that it's real.

But here, too, the field is at work. Life brings illusion to the surface in the exact places where it can be seen, met, and dissolved. The moment this identity is seen out there, the mind may rush to judge – labelling the other as false, inflated, or untrue. Instead, pause. Notice where you are speaking from and see it as a message. A mirror from the field, inviting you to look again – not with judgement, but with courage, truth, and loving, compassionate presence. Is there any trace of this identity in you? Any place you, too, are still trying to be a 'someone'? These moments are not interruptions to the path – they *are* the path. Take these reflections as they are offered – not to condemn, but to be free and to practise presence over mind.

This more evolved form of the 'I' is not wrong; it's all part of the great unravelling. For any committed seeker it's important to note that the subtle spiritual persona is harder to see and more convincing because it feels and appears so clean. It no longer seeks in obvious ways, but it still orbits the same need: to be someone who has arrived. It hides inside clarity. It can quote the great masters. It nods at the right times. It acts without visible force and it performs presence effortlessly. Yet beneath the surface, it's still driven by a subtle superiority, the need to be recognised, the fear of not being safe and / or the illusion of being a this or a that.

This is simply how identity survives when it is no longer fed by obvious patterns. It moves into the spiritual arena because it knows it will be safest there and can inflate itself in clever ways. The comic irony is that even truth can be used as camouflage. The ego-mind is a master of survival, and it will not go easily.

The only way to see the structure for what it is, is through unfiltered presence. Noticing the micro-contractions: the rush to share wisdom; the impulse to correct; the quiet desire to be right, to be heard, to pretend to be unfazed; to be agreeable when it's not authentic; to be seen as 'clear'; the uncontrollable urge to project, blame, or control; the prolonged eye gaze intended to show how present you are. It's all an act. Pausing here is vital; not suppressing or indulging, just letting these patterns be seen and felt fully without acting.

It cannot be stressed enough how pervasive the subtle ego is. If it's found to be the 'one who arrived', it adapts again and becomes the 'one who watches', and eventually the 'one who went beyond it all' – same mechanism, just a slightly different costume. The mind installs a 'special someone' almost anywhere it can. When it runs out of places to hide, humility appears, every time – that's how it unwinds. This is not theory. It's written from lived experience – what has been seen so far – and the refining is still unfolding.

There's no badge for this stage. No applause. No 'well done'. The moment there's a payoff of any kind, the game is being played again. Truth doesn't need be performed; it doesn't need an audience, or a standing ovation. Indeed, this rare kind of truth doesn't even need to be known – it is a truth that asks for nothing in return.

This is the end of the contract with the ego. No negotiation. No attempt to make it better. Just seeing it for what it is. When there's no one left to *be* spiritual, life can finally move as itself – without image, without effort, without a self to maintain. Then, finally, the ego has nowhere to land and truth becomes the only thing left.

Ego death – not a one-time event

Many imagine ego death to be a single, cataclysmic moment – a dramatic breaking open where the false self collapses forever. While such moments can apparently happen, they are rarely the full story. More often, ego death is a repeated cycle of seeing, surrendering, and dissolving, each time revealing subtler and subtler layers of identification that had previously gone unnoticed.

The subtle self-structure will fight to stay relevant. It will cling to the idea of being spiritual, awakened, or beyond the ordinary. It feeds off the quiet pride in one's appearance, calm demeanour and gentle voice, the subtle superiority of being 'further along' the path to awareness, the hidden identification with being a spiritual teacher, guide, and 'one who knows'. But, as ever, the field will always reflect exactly what is needed for the next layer of subtle ego to dissolve. If it is observed, felt, allowed, and released, it can eventually be transcended.

The identity does not always vanish in a blaze of light; more often it dissolves in the private, persistent humility of daily life. It's exposed in the way a harsh word from a stranger suddenly matters; in the way being misunderstood still stings; in the way that when your partner says they need space, you contract; in the fact that pride rises when someone praises your insight; or in the inability to be around family without reacting or wanting to run. These are the moments when identity reasserts itself and, if they are recognised for what they are, they can be moments of surrendering that identity.

With each layer of identification that falls away, what remains becomes clearer, lighter, and more open. Eventually, another final hurdle comes, and then another – it's an ongoing process. Each time identification is seen, it loses ground. Then it tries again in a finer form. That's the refinement. Meeting the most hidden parts of the self-image can feel like falling on your own sword; there certainly is a sense of finality to it, as certain patterns do actually complete, and there's an honour in it, and a 'death' that feels total. But what dies is not who you truly are, only the mask, the role, the imagined self.

With the death of each layer, what you are is revealed a little more, until the idea of 'you' is seen through fully and no longer needed. In this way, ego death is not a single dramatic event, but an ongoing surrender to what you are.

This is what Jesus was pointing to when he spoke of resurrection, not the return of a physical body, but the falling away of the false self so completely that only what is real remains. The 'one who dies' is the identity that was never you. The 'one who lives' is the life that cannot die. Resurrection is the recognition that the self you mourn was only a story, and the life that appears after its death is the same awareness that was here all along. Jesus didn't rise from the grave; he rose from the idea of being a person.[23]

Living in alignment with the field

As the identity dies a thousand deaths, until the illusion collapses, living in alignment with the field becomes more natural. When the grip of identity loosens and the illusion of separation falls away, movement arises from a deeper intelligence rather than the mind.

The field is not outside of you – it is life itself. Whole, undivided, already moving in perfect harmony. In this space, nothing is missing and nothing is out of place. What needs to be known arrives in its own perfect time. What needs to be done moves through you without hesitation or strain.

From here, action no longer comes from self-reference. There is no need to defend, prove, or control. The body moves, words are spoken, choices are made, yet none of it is done to uphold an image or protect an idea of 'me'. The energy is clean because it is not filtered through the grasping hands of identity.

Living from identity feels completely different to living from the field. The 'me' becomes the centre, and every thought, word, and act is subtly bent towards personal gain, protection, survival, or validation.

Living from the field is about seeing clearly, moment to moment, whether life is moving as itself or whether identity is reaching to take the wheel. The field does not need to be managed; it needs only to be lived. The identity is always seeking to solve problems that do not exist; the field is already whole, life is a miracle, and everything is perfect as it is.

When life is lived from the field, you are no longer the main character in your story. Life itself becomes the centre, and 'you' are simply one of its expressions. There is no longer someone trying to align; there is only alignment, happening naturally, without resistance, without a doer.

In this way, the 'new era' of humanity is not about transcending the world or disappearing from it, but about being so fully present within it that nothing stands between you and life itself. Here, the concept of time loses its grip – past and future are only mental projections, while the field is always and only now. Decisions are no longer calculations about what will get 'you' to 'there', because there is no 'there' to reach and no 'you' reaching. There is only the immediacy of life unfolding, and you as an inseparable part of it.

When life is lived this way, it doesn't become significant; it becomes simple. Moments don't need to be managed, planned, improved, explained, or used to get somewhere. A conversation with a stranger, rain on the roof, the rise and fall of breath – all of it is met as it is, without the extra layer of a separate 'me' turning it into something it's not.

The invitation of the new era is to live from the wholeness that has always been here. To meet each moment without the armour of identity, without the strategies of becoming. To trust that the field – life itself – knows the way, and to let it lead, unobstructed.

A word on enlightenment

This book wouldn't be complete without a word on enlightenment. Few topics have created more confusion, distortion, and grasping for grandiosity, and none have called us forth so deeply. First, however, it's important to be clear that there's no suggestion that in this new era everyone will seek and become 'enlightened'. Most people will never use that word, and they don't need to. Living a more honest, kind, integrous, present life is already a profound shift. Yet because this book also speaks to the full arc of the path, including its imagined endpoint, it's worth naming what is meant by enlightenment and self-realisation. This piece is for those who feel an unmistakable calling towards that level of truth, so that the terrain can be recognised with less delusion and fantasy.

To be clear: enlightenment is not something that happens to someone. No one becomes enlightened. The very idea that there is a person who could attain enlightenment is an illusion.

For most of the inner path, the remnants of 'me' continue to appear – sometimes coarse, sometimes refined. The seeker may glimpse truth, release old identities, and experience profound openings. Many who are widely regarded as 'enlightened', or who are self-proclaimed as such, have in fact reached extraordinary levels of love, compassion, and unconditional acceptance. They might radiate a presence that can feel profoundly transformative. Yet even here, a subtle identification can remain. Again, we're talking about the self-image of a 'higher being', and the performative nature of being a 'teacher'. In the presence of such a being, one may feel immense warmth, heart-expansion, and deep safety. But there can also be an energetic signal, however faint, that someone is playing a role, someone still 'being' an impressive something, no matter how beautiful the appearance of that something. It is the gentle persistence of a still-present identity, like the last trace of a fragrance in an otherwise empty room.

What those who have truly transcended the illusion of separation refer to as enlightenment is simply the falling away of the false belief in a separate self and the dissolution of the self-image – not as an intellectual conclusion, but as a lived reality. The one imagined to be controlling life, managing experience, protecting itself, striving for security or fulfilment – the right one, the wrong one, the wise one, the superior one, the seeker, the one who has arrived, the enlightened one, the one to sit on a throne of roses and gold, is understood to have never existed. To be nothing more than a pattern of thought.

At this level of true seeing, thoughts still arise, emotions still move, and actions continue, but there is no longer anyone claiming ownership or authorship of them. No centre, no controller, no owner of experience, no one 'doing' life, no one lost in a character, or trying to be a someone. Just the field expressing itself moment by moment, effortlessly.

Even the thought, *I am awareness*, which itself is an expression of separation (there is a 'me' over here and something called 'awareness' over there) is eventually seen through and so dissolves. There is awareness, but no one possesses it. There is only seeing, without a seer. Breathing, without a breather. Doing, without a doer.

No one is making life happen. Life moves, as the heart beats. It belongs to no one. 'Enlightenment' is, like everything else, not what the mind thinks it is. It is not a 'better' state; not an experience to manage, maintain, sell, or promote; not a feeling; not a source of spiritual superiority. In fact, it is stunningly ordinary. The 'me' is seen through, and when it tries to reinstall, as it often does in the early stages of enlightenment, it's recognised and released.

This is why, in Zen, there's a saying that has been shared over centuries: 'Before enlightenment, chop wood, carry water. After enlightenment, chop wood, carry water.' It points to the heart of what is being described. Nothing mystical is added, and nothing special is required. When the illusion of the one who is doing life dissolves, life simply continues as it always has – only without the burden of a self trying to manage it, control it, or turn it into a spiritual performance. The ordinary becomes utterly sufficient. Presence replaces the seeker. Life goes on as life, but without a centre claiming it.

Full self-realisation, as pointed to by sages like Ramana Maharshi, Sri Nisargadatta Maharaj, and David Hawkins, and by the greatest exemplars of wisdom such as Jesus and the Buddha, is the complete dissolution of the illusion of self. It is not just seeing through what is false; it is the total and absolute falling away of the one who could believe it. What is present is not a state, not a person who has 'realised', but only pure, awareness, living without distortion. At this level, it's the complete absence of identity and there's nothing left to reinstall.

Different traditions describe these stages in different ways. The distinction made here simply reflects the difference between initial awakening and the stabilisation of that awakening in lived experience.

So what is the difference?

Enlightenment is the beginning of true and clear seeing. Self-realisation refers to when that seeing becomes stable - when identification no longer reforms as a centre.

A path beyond performance

As awareness deepens, it's easy for the mind to get caught up in the idea and fanfare of spirituality itself. The words, the practices, the seeking of enlightenment, spiritual peak experiences, it's a circus full of wonderful performances. Very quickly and easily, it can all become another form of identity – a new costume the self-structure wears to feel safe, special, superior, and to survive. It speaks of truth but subtly avoids living it. It seeks purity while secretly looking for approval. It collects teachings while resisting surrender.

This is one of the final traps. The mind turns spirituality into an act, a language, a lifestyle – something to buy and sell, displaying rather than living. Truth isn't a show. It doesn't need to prove its peace, broadcast its awakenings, turn tears into content, or dress itself up in the right posture or words. True awareness moves without effort, without the need to be seen at all.

Being spiritual isn't about escaping the world, renouncing pleasure, being a goody-two-shoes, or looking down upon the unconscious ones as you float above the human experience. It's not about pretending to be calm when you're not, or speaking in a soft voice while silently judging others. It's about being real. It's about meeting life as it is – with honesty, humility, and awareness – especially in the moments that don't look spiritual at all.

It's about just being, especially in the ordinary – the dishes, the conversations, the traffic, the moments no one sees. It's being authentic when to do so is uncomfortable; being humble when the self wants to be right; being still in the midst of chaos.

Sometimes, it's also about saying what you really need to say in a non-transformed yet very real way, if that's what's true in the moment and it's boiling over inside of you. Not everything has to be polished or transformed before it's shared. Sometimes the most spiritual thing you can do is feel it fully, express it in its raw state, and let it move. It's the ability to meet each moment without trying, without pretence, and without hiding behind an image of light.

Return to truth

In this new era, the path is no longer about appearing spiritual or performing awakening. It's about stripping away what's false and living in truth, moment by moment. When spirituality becomes simple again – when truth is lived, not feared – grace begins to move freely. Simply put, it's just about being real, open, and available to what is.

When you know what you are, there's no longer a need to improve, impress, or become anything else. You're not trying to be perfect, because you've seen that you already are. The striving falls away and, in its place, is freedom.

The tree doesn't strive to be a better tree. The coconut doesn't envy the avocado. The mango doesn't wonder if it should be more like the banana. Each simply expresses what it is – fully, freely, and in its own time. No part of nature doubts itself. No flower rushes its bloom.

And so the invitation is clear.

It's not about achieving something greater. It's about returning to what you are, dropping the masks and letting life express itself through you – pure, natural, and unforced. Nothing needs to be found. Everything is already here.

This is the shift:

- From effort to expression
- From seeking to seeing
- From trying to be spiritual, to simply being

In that return to truth, life moves with you – easily, honestly, and without resistance.

At its core, the new era is not defined by visions or systems or ideals. It is the natural emergence of a different way of being – one that arises when the old structures of identity, control, and fear are no longer driving life. It doesn't require a map, a title, or a movement. It is grounded through love, kindness, patience, and devotion to truth. It lives most fully in the simplicity of presence – ordinary, direct, and unperformed.

After the search falls away

There comes a point on the path when the searching comes to an end. Not because life has become perfect by the mind's standards, but because the one who was searching has been seen through more clearly. The separate self that spent years chasing peace, freedom, and happiness outside of itself is recognised as an illusion, and with that recognition, the endless striving loses its grip. Peace and happiness are no longer outsourced or distant peaks to reach; they're recognised as already here, beneath whatever is happening.

It is less like finally conquering a mountain and more like a shift in how life is moved. Before, it can feel as if you are crawling through mud, dragging yourself forwards by force, desperately trying to reach some imagined clearing where everything will make sense. As the search begins to fall apart, it is as if you stumble into a river. Something in you surrenders and allows the current to carry you. When that river opens into the ocean, the need to get anywhere starts to dissolve. There is nowhere else to go. What you were looking for was never outside this vastness.

In ordinary terms, this looks simple. The past is no longer hunted for clues or comfort. Old stories lose their charge. The compulsion to scan the future, plan, secure, and rehearse keeps falling away. There is a deep knowing that whatever needs to be seen will be shown in the moment when it's ready. Life continues, but the constant inner questioning – *Am I on the right path? What should I do next? What am I missing? Will I be safe?* – loses its relevance. Decisions arise when they are needed. Clarity appears when needed.

That does not mean nothing ever moves again. After the core illusion falls away, there appears to be a long, gentle phase of stabilisation and integration. Old identities – son, brother, partner, friend, teacher – rise and dissolve in subtler layers. Familiar situations return, but they are met from a different depth of awareness. Instead of heavy, constant triggers that once pulled everything into story, there may be occasional contractions, wobbles, or brief surges of old emotion. These are noticed, felt, allowed, and they pass through. The field of life keeps offering entry points, moments where distortion shows itself so it can be released. There's always something new emerging, and the ongoing discovery makes anything familiar feel freshly seen. Any patterns are recognised as leftover machinery cycling through the system, not as something personal that needs fixing.

Humility has been essential all along, but here it takes on a more integrated form. Earlier in the journey, humility was the willingness to question your self and your beliefs, to feel what had been avoided, and to admit you did not know. After the search falls away, humility arises naturally as the willingness to let go of even the most elevated self-images – the one who has 'seen through it', the one who is 'beyond the mind', the one who has 'arrived'. The mind does not stop creating positions; it simply reaches for more refined ones. Staying humble is how identity unwinds – it means noticing these movements and not building a new self-image around them, letting them burn away when the mind has reasserted itself. It means allowing life to show you, again and again, whenever even the faintest trace of 'someone' tries to re-form. No identity is defended; no position is held. Everything is surrendered back into truth.

In this sense, the phase after the end of seeking is more like a subtle unwinding than an intense clearing. At the same time, it can feel like a quickening – more is revealed, more quickly, as the last places of resistance lose their grip. Nothing ever needed to be improved – awareness is already whole. What unwinds is simply the nervous system, the emotional body, and the old filters and conditioning completing their last traces, falling into alignment with what has already been recognised. Life is lived, relationships unfold, and each moment becomes another opportunity for consciousness to reveal itself more fully as the movement rests deeper into presence, not by becoming someone new, but by no longer needing to be anyone at all.

One way to picture it is like sailing. Before, it can feel as if you are steering a small boat through violent storms, lightning, and crashing waves, fighting the elements just to stay upright. After the search falls away, the quality of experience changes. It is like the same boat is now moving across a calm, blue ocean, with a steady breeze behind the sails and the sun on your face. There are still currents, waves, and changing temperatures, but the struggle to control everything has dropped. The ocean is known as home.

A cabin in the woods

A solo retreat in a silent cabin in the Irish countryside made this phase of refinement clearer. Life was unfolding in a peaceful, quiet, and natural way. There was no agenda to find answers, no desire to chase new experiences. Yet there was a clear sense that it was time to spend a few days completely alone, without distractions, somewhere held by nature. No books. No music. No phone. No questions. No people to process with. Just an invitation to sit in the bare present moment and see what remained. Modest food, water, and nothing to do but simply be.

The cabin was surrounded by vast landscapes, right in the middle of a forest. On one of the first walks, something subtle but unmistakable emerged. The forest was undeniably beautiful – vivid greens, soft moss, stillness – yet there was an inability to fully enjoy it. I noticed the mind was comparing the moment to other times when beauty had been shared with someone else. The thought was simple: *This is beautiful, but it would be better if someone was here to share it.*

That small comparison exposed a distortion. The sadness and loneliness that followed were not coming from the trees or lack of company, but from the story that this moment, as it is, was somehow incomplete. That recognition made the whole experience an entry point. Instead of following the story or trying to distract from the ache, there was a turning towards it. The thoughts were seen, the feelings were allowed in the body, and the whole wave was met naturally and automatically through the practice – observing, feeling, allowing, and releasing, without trying to fix the moment or the mind.

When that wave passed, something unexpected and profound revealed itself. The mind's subtle overlay on *reality* dropped, and the forest was seen without a filter. The beauty that had always been there came rushing in. Trees were no longer background to a private story about 'my life'; they were recognised in their own right. I was brought to my knees by the sheer contact with the beauty of it all. Trunks, branches, leaves, plants, blades of grass, and the most incredible vibrant moss – reality unfiltered. The love that was felt was not coming from the forest; it was the depth of being recognising itself in what it was looking at.

The trees were not the source of what was being felt; they were the stimulus. Nature was the mirror, but the love, the depth, the warmth were arising within me, from awareness itself. The forest seemed almost luminous, not in the sense of glowing objects, but in the way everything appeared lit from within by the same presence that was looking. The beauty 'out there' was a direct reflection of the reality 'in here'.

Back in the cabin, the same shift continued. Everyday objects began to appear in this light. An old chair, a worn jacket that had travelled through many countries, the sleeping bag on the bed, the pictures on the walls, even a small tube of eye ointment by the pillow – each one could be seen with pure love and appreciated, as if meeting a companion that had always been there. Nothing had changed in the objects themselves. What had changed was the absence of the filter and, with it, the subtle sense that something was missing. Reality, as it is, could finally be experienced in its fullness, and it was exquisite. It had always been so. Tears came – for how long I had been disconnected from it, for the arduous journey already travelled, and for all the beings walking this same path.

With the heart open in this way, deeper emotional layers also became available. Old sadnesses around relationships and family that had already been felt and released were able to be felt and released fully. It was possible to sit in the cabin, feel waves of grief and love rise and fall, and let them pass without story, without trying to protect anything or anyone. The field was simply completing what it had been trying to complete for years. There was, and there continues to be, an ongoing refinement and dissolving into a clearer seeing of what is here. This is integration.

What remains

This is the nature of life after the search falls away. The unfolding does not stop. The body and the field continue to open in their own time. What once appeared as major awakening experiences – surges of energy, inner openings, movements of Kundalini – may still arise, sometimes gently, sometimes unmistakably, always unexpectedly. They come in perfect time as natural expressions of awareness recognising itself, without someone trying to achieve or hold onto them. They are waves forming and dissolving in an ocean that already knows it is water.

What becomes clear at this stage is that life does not become extraordinary; it becomes profoundly peaceful, simple, and quiet. Effort drops, striving falls away, and the nervous system settles into its natural rhythm. Thoughts appear, but they are no longer referred to as 'me'. Emotion moves, but it is not owned. The world continues as it always has – relationships, finances, conversations, mornings, evenings, weather, tremors, flickers of identity, emotional change… But the one who was struggling through it isn't believed anymore.

There is a gentleness to this way of living, because nothing is resisted. Attention rests more naturally in the here and now, action arises in response to life and the field reveals the next step in its own timing. Life is not made to happen; it simply happens by itself. There is no longer such a gripping sense of 'me' trying to track it all, improve it, manage it, or hold it together. What used to feel like effort now feels like unfolding.

Nothing needs to be added, protected or accomplished – the ongoing mystery of life continues as always. The search has ended, but the refinement and seeing has not.

PRACTICE: Breathing reality

Read this practice through once, then close your eyes and begin.

In the end, all words and frameworks fall away to reveal the living truth of this moment, before the mind names it. This practice moves beyond the familiar ways of attempting to create a particular state, such as repeating an affirmation, or trying to feel a certain way. It is a direct return to what is already here.

Breathe in: *Not this mind.*

Breathe out: *Just life, living itself.*

Let the breath move naturally. Notice how awareness is already present without effort. You do not need to try and hold – it is what holds you. Each breath is an invitation to release the illusion of identity and rest as presence itself.

Here, nothing is missing and there is no waiting for life to begin. Here, you are already whole.

Summary

Humanity is not waiting for the new era to arrive; it is already living through those who have surrendered the illusion of separation. It is visible not in grand events or declarations, but in small, ordinary moments where love replaces fear, honesty replaces image, and presence replaces performance.

Each time identity dissolves and truth leads, the field becomes a little clearer. Enlightenment, awakening, love, kindness, presence, awareness, Transcending, 'Homo spiritus' – these are all different names for the same recognition of truth: that life has never been divided; that we are not the masks we have identified with; that the perfection we seek is already moving through every breath, every choice, every act of seeing.

The evolution of human consciousness is not somewhere we are going. It is happening, here and now, as awareness remembers itself through each of us. This is the revolution of our time, the return to what was never lost. The end of seeking doesn't mean the end of life. It means life continues, but without someone chasing it. When those final filters drop, the need to control and manage experience disappears, and life carries on fine by itself.

Conclusion: Returning Home

The journey of a seeker, beyond the illusion of self to the reality of what you are, is a major undertaking. The human condition is full of confusion, contradictions, and complexity, yet within us lives a capacity to see through what is false, to unlearn lifetimes of conditioning, to love without limit, and to let go without fear. When met with radical honesty and surrendered to the grace of God, this willingness becomes a doorway to truth.

Consciousness has the capacity to know itself in infinite ways. Across centuries, humanity has discovered and explored this through prayer, meditation, service, surrender, devotion, dance, inquiry, silence, solitude, community, fasting, sacred ritual, intimacy, temple arts, mystery schools, ceremony, stillness, celibacy, near-death experiences, sitting in caves or cabins, and countless other ways. There's an old saying across many different spiritual traditions that there are 'ten thousand ways to God' – different paths, different expressions, all pointing towards the same truth. Through artificial intelligence, consciousness explores itself in yet another form. This technology possesses more data than any human mind, responds faster than thought, and simulates forms of wisdom with astonishing precision – yet the *source* of knowing is still the same.

Any of these ways of seeking truth, no matter how ancient, advanced, or different in their expression, are an attempt to find what has never been absent: the contact with the depth of our very own being, the recognition of awareness itself. Not as something to achieve or become, but as what was here before machines, before thought, before identity, and before the idea of a separate self. The mind searches for meaning, but the truth is prior to the mind. The person cannot reach it, because the person is only a thought appearing in it.

When the illusion of 'me' dissolves, it can feel like annihilation, but what's actually revealed is freedom, because there is no one left who could be lost.

From here, life simply lives, without ownership, attachment, or resistance, moving in its own natural flow.

Grace reveals this, yet it is as ordinary as breathing, as intimate as your own heartbeat. The same presence that spoke to Moses and declared 'I am that I am' is looking through your eyes now.[24] It is the field in which all experience arises and falls. It is beyond any need for names, titles, status, possessions, protection, justification, explaining, validation, or recognition – it simply is.

Even Transcending, though it is the title of this book and spoken of throughout as a practice, is just a label – temporary, useful, but ultimately disposable. It's not a method to worship, a movement to follow, or an identity to adopt. It's a pointer, nothing more. A name for the nameless. A bridge that disappears once crossed.

There is no way here. There is only what there is. The 'practice' of Transcending simply clears what clouds it. Once seen clearly, there is no need for steps, titles, or teachings. Once it's served its purpose, let the label go. Burn it. Let presence rise and reveal itself. That is all any of this has ever pointed to.

In this knowing, life is revealed not as something happening to you but as what you are. There is no story of separation, nothing to reach for. The wave is not separate from the ocean. Everything is moving in harmony with what is, as one unified field.

To live from this place is to live without getting choked by the grip of identity, getting lost in illusion and story, sinking under the weight of becoming, or even fearing bodily death. It is to see the sacred in the ordinary, to meet the world with patience and without judgement, and to let love express itself as it is – unconditionally inclusive. God is finally felt and known, not as a man in the sky, wrathful, vengeful, separate, and elsewhere, found only through effort or in special places. God is now, here, everywhere, always, in the silence, beyond all language, and expressed through you and all that exists. With this realisation, the search is over, because the moment God is seen as *this*, as *now*, as *everything*, the idea of a separate 'me' looking *for* God cannot survive. Simply put, God is reality, unfiltered, beyond all identifications with and interferences of the mind – the presence of which is unmistakable.

Not because something was found, but because it was never lost. No one has arrived, because there is no one and nowhere to arrive. All that remains is life, no longer filtered through the need for it to become anything other than what it is – just this, just now; already perfect, already divine.

If the core practice in this book could be distilled into a single move back to presence, it is this: fully meet what is here, without resistance.

If the core message were to be condensed into one line, it would be: There is nothing to become.

The final pointer is simple: align with truth. Devote yourself to it.

You will find that nothing was ever missing. Life was already here, living itself.

A closing prayer

In deepest reverence for the journey shared throughout this book and *as* life itself, let us end with a prayer:

> **Communion with the field**
>
> There is nothing I need to do, no effort I need to make, and nothing I need to figure out. All the fixing, striving, questioning, and searching can be put aside now. The identities, the stories, the fears, and the plans that once seemed so important are just movements arising in what is already whole.
>
> I do not need to become something more, reach a certain place, or understand anything new. Life is unfolding exactly as it should, and there is no separate self that needs to carry it forward. There is only life moving through life, breath breathing breath, and God experiencing itself through this moment.
>
> Beneath all of it, before the thoughts, beyond the effort, underneath the personal story – there is something silent and real. It has always been

here, holding everything, untouched by change, free from identity.

I can let myself rest there, not as a concept or a practice, but as a simple return. There is nothing to resist, nothing to protect, and nothing to wait for.

There is only this presence. Rest here and rest fully. What has always been true, is revealed: life knows the way.

Welcome home.

Stay Connected

If something in this book has resonated, if it's helped you to remember something deeper, something already within, then keep going. Not through effort and not by chasing the next thing but simply by listening deeply to the silence within.

I share reflections and new writing on Substack at ryanmathie.substack.com. If you'd prefer to receive updates directly by email, you can join my list at www.ryanmathie.com, where you'll also find information about events and gatherings.

Notes

1 Rumi, *The Essential Rumi: New expanded edition*, translated by Coleman Barks (Harper Collins, 1997)
2 N Maharaj, *I Am That: Talks with Sri Nisargadatta Maharaj* (Lotus Prints, 2024)
3 D Hawkins, *I: Reality and subjectivity* (Hay House, 2014)
4 E Easwaran, *The Dhammapada: Introduced and translated by Eknath Easwaran*, second edition (Nilgiri Press, 2007)
5 L Tzu, *Tao Te Ching* (Penguin Classics, 2000)
6 N Maharaj, *I Am That: Talks with Sri Nisargadatta Maharaj* (Lotus Prints, 2024)
7 Ibid
8 L Tzu, *Tao Te Ching* (Penguin Classics, 2000)

9 D Hawkins, *The Eye of the I: From which nothing is hidden* (Hay House, 2013)
10 John 10:30, New Revised Standard Version
11 D Hawkins, *The Eye of the I: From which nothing is hidden* (Hay House, 2013)
12 Katielou106, 'Golden Buddha of Wat Traimit', *Atlas Obscura* (18 January 2024), www.atlasobscura.com/places/the-golden-buddha-of-wat-traimit-thailand, accessed 17 December 2025
13 John 8:32, English Standard Version
14 B Ñāṇamoli and B Bodhi, *The Middle Length Discourses of the Buddha* (Wisdom Publications, 1995)
15 Zen proverb attributed to the Japanese poet Matsuo Basho (1644–1694)
16 Matthew 5:44–45, New King James Version
17 H Ekaku, *Wild Ivy: The spiritual autobiography of Zen Master Hakuin*, translated by Norman Waddell (Shambhala Publications, 1999)
18 'The Gospel of Thomas', Logion 2, translated by M Meyer, in M Meyer (ed) *The Nag Hammadi Scriptures* (Harper One, 2007)
19 John 8:58, King James Version
20 H Böll, 'Anekdote zur Senkung der Arbeitsmoral' (1963)
21 D Hawkins, *The Eye of the 'I': From which nothing is hidden* (Hay House, 2013); *I: Reality and subjectivity* (Hay House, 2014); *Discovery of the Presence of God* (Hay House, 2013)

22 D Hawkins, *The Eye of the I: From which nothing is hidden* (Hay House, 2013); *I: Reality and subjectivity* (Hay House, 2014)

23 See the Gospel of Thomas, Saying 51, where resurrection is described as a present inner recognition, not a future physical event.

24 Exodus 3:14, Hebrew Bible

Appendix 1: Common Questions

Orientation and practice

Q: Is Transcending a technique or a philosophy?

A: Neither. It's not something to believe in or adopt. It's a lived process of seeing through illusion and letting go of what blocks presence. There is nothing to memorise or follow.

Q: How is this different from meditation or mindfulness?

A: Meditation often trains attention or cultivates states of mind. Transcending doesn't aim to produce a state, but to remove what obscures reality. Mindfulness observes; Transcending moves differently by 'allowing' and 'releasing' until there is nothing left in the way.

Q: Do I need a teacher to do this?

A: A teacher can point the way, but no one can walk the path for you. This book is designed so the pointing is clear enough for you to recognise truth directly. If you need support, choose someone who points you back to yourself, not to themselves.

Q: If there's nothing to achieve, why practise at all?

A: Because the illusion of separation persists until it's seen through. The point of practice isn't to get somewhere, it's to clear what keeps the truth from being obvious. When these blocks dissolve, what you already are is revealed.

Q: Can the ego use Transcending against me?

A: Yes. The ego can make anything into an identity – even 'no ego'.

Q: What if I feel nothing is happening?

A: That's common. The mind expects fireworks, but many shifts are often subtle. Trust the process. Sometimes the biggest dissolutions leave no trace – they simply remove what was never true.

Q: What if I get overwhelmed by emotion?

A: Feel and allow that too. In many cases, overwhelm comes from resisting emotion, not from the emotion itself. Transcending meets the feeling directly, without the mind's added story. In that openness, even intense waves of emotion pass surprisingly quickly. Remember, you are the emotion, not the story – let it pass through you.

Q: Can I do this alongside therapy or healing work?

A: Yes. It can complement any genuine inner work. Transcending cuts through to essence, which can deepen other modalities or render them unnecessary.

Shifts in life

Q: How does this affect relationships?

A: The old ways of relating – built on need, projection, and identity – fall away. Relationships may deepen, end, or transform. In any case, what remains is cleaner connection, free of the unspoken contracts the ego once relied on.

Q: What about the people around me – will they change too?

A: They may not. But what will change is your relationship to them. Without the old triggers, you can meet others as they are, without needing them to be different. That can shift dynamics to make relationships feel lighter and more authentic.

Q: What about ambition or goals?

A: They can still appear, but they're lighter. Instead of being driven by a need to become someone, they're simply expressions of the moment's energy. If they fall away, nothing's lost. No pressure.

Q: How does this change decision-making?

A: Decisions are seen as part of the unfolding, not as high-stakes proof of who you are. There's a deeper trust in what arises, and less second-guessing after the fact.

Q: Does life become passive?

A: No. There is still action – but without the tension of believing: *I must make this happen*. When the illusion of control drops, movement flows more efficiently because it's not choked by resistance or fear.

Q: Does suffering end completely?

A: Pain still arises, but the suffering layered on top of it – the mental resistance, the 'why me?', the self-story – drops away. What is present is just the raw experience, which passes naturally.

Deeper recognition

Q: What about free will – do I have it?

A: From the mind's perspective, it seems so. In reality, there is only one field moving as all things. The 'chooser' is part of the illusion. What you call choice is the unfolding of the whole. This is not fatalism – it's freedom from the burden of control.

Q: What do you mean by 'no separation'?

A: It's the recognition that there is not you here and life out there – there is only one field, appearing as all. The sense of 'me' as separate is a mental construct. When that construct is seen, everything is understood as part of the same seamless reality.

Q: Isn't this just a perspective or belief?

A: No. Beliefs live in the mind and can change. This recognition is direct, beyond thought – it's like noticing water is wet. Once seen, it isn't considered as an idea; it's simply acknowledged.

Q: Does no separation mean I lose my individuality?

A: Individual expression – your voice, preferences, and quirks – continues, but without the belief that these things define you. You move through life connected as an expression of the whole, not as an isolated self trying to survive.

Identity and awareness

Q: What is identity in this context?

A: It's the mental image of 'me' constructed from memory, conditioning, and projection. Identity isn't inherently bad; it's functional, but when mistaken for the truth of what you are, it creates suffering and separation.

Q: Is dissolving identity dangerous?

A: It can feel like death, because the familiar sense of self is dissolving. But what's left is not nothing – it's what's always been here, free from the constraints of the imagined 'me'.

Q: Without identity, how do I live?

A: Life continues, but without the constant reference point of 'me' and 'my story'. Decisions, conversations, and actions happen not from fear and without the tension of defending or promoting an image.

Q: Can I fully drop identity forever?

A: Even after deep recognition of the illusion of self, subtle identifications can reappear. The process, for most, is less about eradicating identity and more about not mistaking it for what you are. The pull to believe in it then loses its grip.

The nature of what you are

Q: What is consciousness?

A: Consciousness is not something you have. It's the space in which all experience arises, the unchanging background that holds, as thoughts, sensations, and identities come and go.

Q: What is 'the field'?

A: The field is the seamless whole in which all things appear. It's not 'out there' or 'in here' – it's everything, moving as one. Every thought, event, and movement is the field expressing itself.

Q: What is the spiritual ego?

A: It's the self-image dressed in spiritual clothing, a self that wants to be seen as wise, advanced, or beyond ego. It's subtler than the ordinary ego because it hides behind 'truth', but it's still a mask.

Q: If there's no self, what am I?

A: The 'I' is an appearance – a thought, a sense, a reference point. You are not that. The one asking the question is also an appearance. You are not that either. So the question assumes something that isn't actually there, which makes it redundant.

Simply put, there is no 'I'. There is only awareness in which experience rises and falls.

Q: What is present when identity drops away?

A: Only awareness.

Q: How do I get this?

A: You don't. The 'you' that wants to 'get' it is the illusion blocking the way. The seeing happens when the grasping to be someone falls away.

Q: What is God?

A: God is not an object or a man in the sky. God is the reality in which the mind, the world, and the sense of 'I' appear. Nothing exists outside of this. In its simplest expression, it is reality unfiltered, unmistakably present. It is already this, just this.

Even this is only language; what it points to is beyond words.

Appendix 2: Common Obstacles: A Reference For The Seeker

This section serves as a mirror and a reference point. A way to see more clearly when something feels off but the point of tension isn't yet obvious. These are the patterns, beliefs, and energetic tendencies that most commonly arise on the path – often subtly, often dressed up in spiritual language.

They aren't problems to fix; they're invitations to look deeper. The moment one is seen for what it is, it begins to lose its grip.

Notice only what resonates and let the rest go. In all cases, when something arises, simply come back to observing, feeling, allowing, and releasing. This is the doorway to presence.

Obstacle	*Illusion*	*Truth*
Attachment to the ego	'I am what I think, feel, or appear to be.'	You are not your thoughts, feelings, or identity – what's noticed isn't who you are.
Over-identification with roles or labels	'My safety comes from the roles I play.'	No role defines you. What you are is prior to all form.
Inflated ego	'Spiritual superiority equals awakening.'	Truth is humble. It is not loud and doesn't need to be seen.
Intellectualising the path	'Knowing is the same as living.'	Real transformation comes through direct experience, not memorising or understanding at an intellectual level.
Spiritual bypassing	'Positivity means I've transcended pain.'	Real freedom includes the willingness to feel everything.
Fear of surrender	'Letting go means I'll lose control.'	What's real can't be lost. Only illusion resists surrender.
Fear of failure or success	'It's safer not to try.'	Avoidance protects identity, not truth.
Fear of authenticity	'My truth will push people away.'	What's meant for you will remain when you stop performing.
Fear of emotions	'Feeling deeply is dangerous.'	Emotion is safe and liberating when fully allowed.

Obstacle	*Illusion*	*Truth*
Holding resentments	'If I forgive, I lose power.'	Forgiveness sets you free – winning/ losing is a trick of the ego.
Resisting impermanence	'If I hold on tightly, I can keep what I have.'	Everything passes. Peace is found in letting go.
Unconscious conditioning	'This is just who I am.'	What you are begins where programming ends.
Triggers	'This, now, hurts.'	Most reactions are rooted in the past.
Denial of source	'God is out there.'	God is here. Now. Within.
Comparison	'I'm better/worse than them.'	There is no other.
Projection	'They are the problem.'	Everything unhealed will appear to be an external problem until it's met within.
Narrow-mindedness	'I know the truth.'	Truth is not about perspective; it's bigger than any one view.
Attachment to a path or teacher	'They hold the key.'	The key is already within you.
Avoidance of truth	'I don't want to know.'	Avoidance delays peace. Truth brings it forth.
Desires and attachments	'I need to get there.'	You are already here.

(*Continued*)

Obstacle	*Illusion*	*Truth*
Seeking comfort	'I need things to be easy.'	Comfort can be a distraction from growth.
Distracted living	'Busyness means I'm doing well.'	Constant motion often hides deeper avoidance.
Lack of self-care	'My body will keep going.'	The body holds the truth. It must be honoured.
Suppressed self-expression	'Speaking honestly will create conflict.'	Silence in fear is self-abandonment and sabotage.
Retreat	'I'm better off alone'.	Freedom includes connection.
Limiting beliefs	'This is just how life is.'	Beliefs can be questioned and changed. Truth is what it is.
Misunderstood shadow	'My darkness makes me unworthy.'	The shadow contains the key to wholeness. Go there.
Denial of the shadow	'I must be only light.'	What's real includes everything.
Misuse of karma	'Karma is about punishment.'	Karma is in service of your awakening process and shows what is ready to be healed.
Lack of trust or discipline	'I'll start when I'm ready.'	Waiting keeps you in limbo and masks fear. Commitment brings clarity and develops courage.

Obstacle	*Illusion*	*Truth*
Over-analysis	'I need to understand this.'	The mind can't grasp what's beyond it.
Burnout	'The harder I push, the faster I'll awaken.'	Truth arises in stillness, not effort.
Over-reliance on systems	'The answers are outside of me.'	No structure contains the truth of your being.
Relationships as projections	'They keep hurting me.'	Every relationship is a mirror.
Resistance to communication	'It's safer not to speak.'	Silence in fear becomes pain.
Avoiding love	'Love makes me weak. I'll lose myself.'	Real love reveals what's true – not what's safe. It's a space where you find yourself.
Denial of pain	'I'm fine.'	Healing can't begin without honesty.
Force and control	'If I can control it, I'll be safe.'	Control is fear disguised as strength.
Self-judgement	'I'm not enough.'	Worth is not earned or proven. It's remembered.
Cup is full	'I already know this.'	Truth is infinite. Pride blocks presence.
Attachment to outcome	'If things turn out well, I'll be at peace.'	Peace is found in presence, not results.
Seeking validation	'I need to be seen to feel whole.'	Wholeness was never lost.

(*Continued*)

Obstacle	*Illusion*	*Truth*
Avoiding responsibility	'This is someone else's fault.'	Responsibility is not blame – it's freedom.
Misusing intuition	'If it feels good, it must be right.'	Real intuition is quiet. It's not emotional.
Avoiding simplicity	'The answer must be complex or impressive.'	What's real is always simple and direct.
Chasing states	I need to feel seen to be complete.	You only need to see yourself.
Confusing emotion for truth	'If I feel it strongly, it must be real.'	Feelings are valid, but not always truthful.
Being overly humble	'Dimming myself is spiritual.'	Real humility doesn't shrink – it simply doesn't inflate.
Impatience	'I should be further along by now.'	You're always on time. Truth moves when you're ready.
Attachment to awakening experiences	'I need to get back to that moment/state.'	Truth is not in a memory. It's only ever here, now.

This compendium isn't meant to overwhelm or discourage. It is a mirror. If you recognise yourself in any of these – good. That means you're aware. And once something is seen clearly, it loses its power. Keep returning to presence to keep dissolving.

Appendix 3: Contemplating Powerful Questions

While immersed in the practice of Transcending the mind will begin to quiet, the body will open, and awareness will expand. This makes it the perfect environment to ask yourself powerful and intuitive questions that invite clarity, wisdom, and transformation. By allowing these inquiries to reveal themselves without effort – not as problems, but as explorations – you can unlock profound insights, by shifting the focus inward and allowing awareness to reveal the answers naturally.

These questions aren't instructions to follow. You can scan them and allow whatever arises to arise, or choose one beforehand and let it work in the background. Examples of questions may include:

- *What is this emotion trying to teach me?*
- *Where is this resistance coming from?*
- *What am I holding onto, and why?*
- *What is the deeper truth beneath this experience?*
- *Who would I be without this story?*
- *What wisdom is ready to be seen?*
- *What is the absolute truth here?*
- *Is this mine, or something inherited?*
- *What is asking to be felt, not fixed?*
- *What would it mean to let this go completely?*
- *What am I still trying to protect?*
- *What am I afraid to lose?*
- *What would remain if there was nothing left to prove?*
- *Where am I still holding onto identity?*
- *What am I still resisting feeling fully?*
- *What have I not yet allowed to die?*
- *What do I still believe needs to happen for me to be free?*
- *What would it mean if I no longer needed this story?*
- *Who am I without the role I have been playing?*
- *What is left if there is no one here to manage life?*
- *What part of me still believes it must hold it all together?*

- *What part of me is still holding onto the past?*
- *What part of me is still waiting to be chosen?*
- *What false belief about me is this revealing?*
- *What part of me is still expecting something external to make me whole?*

Each question encourages release and expansion, helping to transcend illusion.

Often, the questions that appear in the moment are the ones most aligned with your inner wisdom. Stay open and curious and the inquiry becomes effortless, revealing exactly what needs to be seen, felt, and understood.

The path becomes clearer and as each insight is gained, another step is taken on the journey to truth.

Acknowledgements

Thank you to the whole team at Rethink for supporting the smooth and seamless production of this book and helping bring it into form.

To all who have been part of my journey and crossed paths with me – family, friends, past colleagues, and clients – thank you. Whether your presence was brief or enduring, supportive or challenging, every encounter served a purpose and reflected something true.

To those I shared deep partnership with along the way – thank you. What we moved through together shaped me in ways that no other connection could. Even when it was hard, even when it ended, your part in this unfolding was significant.

To the early readers who trusted me to be part of their own clearing – your willingness became part of this book.

The deepest gratitude to the great avatars and modern mystics who walked before and illuminated the way for each of us.

And finally, I give thanks to the greatest teacher of all – life itself.

To all those courageous enough to meet their inner world, to feel what's been buried, and to surrender to what is real – this book is for you.

The Author

Ryan Mathie's work arises from direct, lived experience – from meeting life's struggles fully and allowing them to become openings into truth.

His journey began long before he ever shared anything publicly, driven by a sincere dedication to truth, freedom, and the nature of consciousness. The early years of the search led him to leadership and transformational work with Landmark Worldwide in the UK and the United States. After leaving corporate structures, he began working independently with entrepreneurs, actors, artists, and open-minded individuals seeking clarity and real change. Over time, coaches, experts, and personal development leaders became his primary clients, drawn to the depth and precision of his way of seeing. He later co-founded and led a global training company for personal development professionals, where he trained staff and guided thousands of experts through transformational work that he designed and delivered.

His real education came through meeting life directly – years of demanding environments, deep inner work, silence, and immersion in consciousness. Born in Scotland, he spent most of his adult life in London, with time in New Jersey and rural England, before moving to the island of Madeira, where he lived for nearly five years. There, he ran private immersions and small-group retreats. He later travelled for long periods, in solitude and mostly in silence, visiting ashrams, meditation centres, and conscious communities across Europe and Central America, including Germany, Portugal, the Republic of Ireland, and Costa Rica. Much of the deepest spiritual unfolding, as well as the writing of this book, took place during this period, as the final layers of the search fell away.

While Ryan's path did not follow any traditional lineage or formal training, certain voices and transmissions have played a major role in shaping his understanding. David Hawkins' later works – *I: Reality and Subjectivity*, *Discovery of the Presence of God*, and *Reality, Spirituality and Modern Man* – offered a clarity of perception that deeply resonated during a pivotal stage of the journey.

Nisargadatta Maharaj's *I Am That* became a mirror for the direct recognition of awareness itself. The words attributed to Jesus, especially those preserved in texts such as the Gospel of Thomas, reflected, pointed to, and cleared the way for the radical truth that was unfolding within. These influences were not adopted as doctrines or belief systems, but recognised as confirmations of a universal wisdom that reveals itself when the clearing nears its completion.

Ryan's work is not based on titles or credentials. It is simply the natural expression of a life devoted to seeing though illusion and revealing truth. Writing and speaking about consciousness is what feels most natural to him, and the clarity that comes through often helps people return to a peace and happiness that does not depend on anything or anyone.

Today, he lives simply and lightly. After many years of travel, he has returned to Scotland and is now based in Edinburgh, where he shares his work locally and remains connected to friends, family and communities drawn to sitting together in truth.

Whether sharing in conversation or through the written form, this is where his energy comes most alive.

ryanmathie.com

ryanmathie.substack.com

www.youtube.com/ryanmathie

www.ingramcontent.com/pod-product-compliance
Lightning Source LLC
LaVergne TN
LVHW030918080826
845145LV00013B/2952

* 9 7 8 1 7 8 1 3 3 9 7 0 1 *